INTELLECTUALS AND ASSASSINS
Writings at the End of Soviet Communism

by Stephen Schwartz

Preface by Roger Kimball

San Francisco-Washington-Sarajevo-Prishtina
1988-2000

INTELLECTUALS AND ASSASSINS

by Stephen Schwartz

Preface by Roger Kimball

ISBN: 1898855 55 2

Produced in the UK
Printed in Hungary
Cover Design by Andrea Daniel, Partners

Anthem Press

Anthem Press is an imprint of the Wimbledon Publishing Company
P.O. Box 9779, London SW19 7QA Fax: (+44) 20 8944 0825
E-mail: sales@wpcpress.com

"True literature can only exist where it is created not by diligent and trustworthy officials but by madmen, misfits, heretics, dreamers, rebels, and sceptics. When a writer must be sensibly and rigidly orthodox... there can only be a paper literature, a pulp literature read today and used for wrapping bars of soap tomorrow."

−Yevgeny Zamyatin

Also by Stephen Schwartz

Incidents in the life of Benjamin Péret, FOCUS, San Francisco, 1981

Brotherhood of the Sea: A History of the Sailors' Union of the Pacific, New Brunswick, Transaction Books, 1986.

The Transition: From Authoritarianism to Democracy in the Hispanic World, San Francisco, ICS Press, 1986 (editor).

Spanish Marxism vs. Soviet Communism: A History of the P.O.U.M., New Brunswick, Transaction Books, 1988 (with Víctor Alba).

A Strange Silence: The Emergence of Democracy in Nicaragua, San Francisco, ICS Press, 1992.

From West to East: California and the Making of the American Mind, New York, The Free Press, 1998.

"A Dishonest 20th Century Comedy," Sarajevo, VKBI, 2000.

Kosovo: Background to a War, London, Anthem Press, 2000.

The Iron Rose: A Balkan Jewish Miscellany, London, Anthem Press, forthcoming.

CONTENTS

FOR DANILO KIŠ

Prishtina, Kosova, 2000

Author's Note:

Places and dates of publication of the essays in this collection indicate their original printing. Some have been expanded since they first appeared.

PREFACE

By Roger Kimball

Hannah Arendt once described totalitarianism as a kind of "experiment against reality." What she had in mind with this arresting phrase was the "curiously varying mixture of gullibility and cynicism" that totalitarian movements both depend upon and inspire: a strange amalgam that encourages susceptible souls to believe "everything and nothing, [to] think that everything was possible and nothing was true." What binds totalitarians together, Arendt wrote, "is a firm and sincere belief in human omnipotence. Their moral cynicism, their belief that everything is permitted, rests on the solid conviction that everything is possible." Looking back at the blood-soaked twentieth century—a century conspicuous for its embrace of large-scale utopian schemes—it is impossible to overlook the results of that infatuation with unlimited possibility. Systematic murder, oppression masquerading as freedom, credulousness dressed up as idealism: the menu of toxic eventualities that have marked mankind's flirtation with totalitarian movements is as long as it is sordid and dispiriting.

Books like Leszek Kolakowski's *Main Currents of Marxism*, Raymond Aron's *The Opium of the Intellectuals,* and Arendt's *The Origins of Totalitarianism* have provided an intellectual anatomy of "the totalitarian temptation" (in Jean-François Revel's phrase); more recent studies like Robert Conquest's *The Great Terror* and Stéphane Courtois's *The Black Book of Communism* have provided up-to-date statistics of the cost in human lives of Communist tyranny ("U.S.S.R.: 20 million deaths, China: 65 million deaths," etc.). Stephen Schwartz's *Intellectuals and Assassins* offers an important supplement to this literature of disenchantment. George Orwell once spoke of ideas so ridiculous that only an intellectual could believe them. It is part of Schwartz's task in *Intellectuals and Assassins* to remind us that ridiculous ideas can also be murderous ones: preposterousness is no bar to malevolence, nor is silliness incompatible with tyranny. Leszek Kolakowski was undoubtedly right when he observed that "the self-deification of mankind" that Marxism implies winds up by revealing "the farcical aspect of human bondage." But, Schwartz reminds us, the Stalinist version of that farce has generally been set in the Gulag or secret police cellar.

Students of totalitarian movements have often remarked on the baffling layer-within-a-layer structure they exhibit. Hannah Arendt compared the organization of totalitarianism to an onion: a seemingly infinite agglomeration of "skins" that, when finally plumbed, reveals an empty center. Hence the frequency with which one finds the "cult of personality" in totalitarian movements: in default of legitimate authority, charisma—even if it is only manufactured charisma, artificially maintained—steps in to fill the gap. Hence, too, the proliferation of rival factions, "enemies of the people," and multifarious intrigues with which totalitarianism regularly confronts us. Not for nothing does the phrase "politically correct" have its origins in totalitarian movements. Believers in utopia—the word, remember, literally means "no place"—find themselves intoxicated by the thought of endless possibility, which often turns out to be indistinguishable from endless treachery. The belief that everything is permissible rests not only on the conviction that everything is possible but also the presumption that everyone is expendable.

Facing up to the real dimensions of this evil has proved to be extraordinarily difficult—partly because the seductive nature of political ideology is felt even by those who have escaped its murderous rage. Indeed, it is not at all clear whether, even at this late hour, Western liberal opinion is prepared to acknowledge either the depth of Communist tyranny or the accessory nature of its own repeated capitulations and fellow-traveling. If the twentieth century has been the most deadly in history, it was also among the most amnesiac.

Intellectuals and Assassins provides a useful antidote to that amnesia, a series of vivid reminders of where the flirtation with Stalinism and its allotropes has taken us. It would be difficult to think of anyone more qualified for this task than Stephen Schwartz. As he reminds us in these pages, he himself was a "red diaper baby." His mother was a member of the Communist Party in Ohio, his father was a fellow traveler. Schwartz therefore has the requisite biographical coefficient: he knows from the inside the appeal, the texture of feeling, of the movements and forces he describes.

"In the world of American Stalinist child-rearing," Schwartz writes, "the truth was the biggest problem; not so much the facts about capitalism and communism—although, God knows, these were sacrificed to ideological imperatives—as truth in a more personal sense. Thus, denials and silences were a regular part of home life: parents often hiding their activities from their children; children being asked to adulate Soviet communism while disclaiming their parents' affiliation with the party. McCarthyism was one reason for these public evasions, but it was often used as a pretext: The party had ordered members to conceal their affiliation even at the height of the ultraradical Depression years."

Schwartz also possesses an encyclopedic knowledge of the many personalities, factions, sub-factions, and splinter groups involved. For anyone not totally immersed in the history of totalitarianism, it is extremely difficult to keep straight the architecture of the totalitarian onion, to remember who is in and out of favor at a particular moment, what treacheries follow from a particular directive or change of policy, to recognize, in Lenin's chilling summary of power politics, "who whom." Schwartz expertly helps us sort through the tangled episodes of twentieth-century totalitarianism and its repercussions. His impressive command of foreign languages gives him access to documents and personalities that would otherwise be inaccessible to most English speakers. He seems to be as at home in Sarajevo or Mexico City as he is in San Francisco or London.

It is easy to see that with this book Stephen Schwartz has made an important and wide-ranging contribution to our understanding of twentieth-century political mendacity. As always, God is in the details. Schwartz has collected here dozens of brief portraits, reviews, responses to news items, and a few longer reflections. The result is a rich mosaic of a book. Schwartz covers everything from the so-called Venona transcripts—the deciphering of some 2,900 secret Soviet communications from 1940-1948 that began to be published in 1994—to various heroes of the left such as the singer Paul Robeson and the novelist Lillian Hellman, both of whom were committed Stalinists.

Today, Robeson is widely portrayed as a victim of "McCarthyism." Where I went to college, there was a music building that was renamed the "Paul Robeson House." We were all told about the sad fate of this brave, talented man who was prevented from working by the nasty agents of Joe McCarthy. In 1998, as part of an effort to get Robeson's likeness on a U.S. postage stamp, 60 members of Congress signed a letter assuring the public that Robeson's "contribution to American society and his personal accomplishments are to be extolled." The lawmakers went on to describe him as "perhaps the only true Renaissance man the 20th century has known." In fact, as Schwartz points out, Robeson was a Soviet apologist who maintained that only in the Soviet Union were blacks really free. At the World Peace Congress in 1949, Robeson publicly declared that American blacks would not fight for the American flag, least of all against Moscow: "It is unthinkable," he said, that his race "would go to war on behalf of those who oppressed us for generations." Russia he described as "a country which in one generation has raised our people to the full dignity of mankind." In the same year, like many other artists under Stalinist "discipline," he voluntarily gave up acting and singing, explaining that "I have no time in the political struggle of today to entertain people." Robeson received the Stalin prize in 1953, the year of the dictator's death, and he signed a eulogy that contained the benediction "Glory to Stalin. Forever will his name be honored and beloved in all lands."

Schwartz is equally good on the loathsome Lillian Hellman whose *Scoundrel Time* helped create the myth that the so-called Hollywood 10 were benign actors and film directors unfairly stigmatized by the House Un-American Activities Committee. But Schwartz reminds us that these people "far from being harmless do-gooders, were hardcore Stalinists" who defended "the Soviet purges, the Hitler-Stalin pact of 1939, and Stalin's postwar aggression". They filled their movies with Soviet propaganda, as in Warner Brothers' 1943 *Mission to Moscow,* "which extolled the purges and slandered Stalin's victims." Hellman was always going on about the "witch hunt" conducted by the U.S. government against alleged Communists. But the real witch hunt, as Schwartz points out, was the attack on anti-Communists by liberals who clung desperately to the illusion of radical "idealism." Schwartz also provides an excellent analysis of *The Secret World of American Communism*, one of the first books to make use of newly opened Soviet archives after the disintegration of the Soviet Union. The book provides indisputable evidence that the Communist Party of the United States of America deployed a comprehensive underground network to recruit spies and conduct various espionage activities on behalf on the former Soviet Union. In other words, *The Secret World of American Communism* completely discredits what the authors called the "prevailing academic consensus" about the nature of the Communist Party of the United States of America. According to that consensus, the CPUSA was merely an impatient version of American liberalism—"democracy in a hurry," as Earl Browder, head of the CPUSA in the 1930s, once put it. A corollary of this view is that American anti-communism in the 1940s and 1950s (and down through the 1980s and 1990s) was little more than a paranoid fantasy—a "nightmare in red," as one historian put it: a McCarthyite witch-hunt that wildly exaggerated, indeed, invented, the alleged Communist threat.

As Schwartz notes, *The Secret World of American Communism* puts paid to that notion forever. In fact, the documents assembled in that book reveal (in the words of one of the editors) "a massive conspiratorial operation" in which "an American political organization sold itself to a totalitarian power." In some cases, they provide hard evidence for things that have long been suspected; in others they reveal entirely new aspects of Communist influence in American life. The book shows, for example, that Soviet subsidies, often in the form of confiscated gold, silver, and jewels, began arriving in the United States as early as 1919. One of the first beneficiaries of that largess was the often-romanticized left-wing journalist John Reed, one of the founders of the American Communist Party who was glamorized by Warren Beatty in the movie *Reds*. The very first document in *The Secret World of American Communism* records the payment to Reed of a subsidy worth more than $1 million—an enormous sum at the time. (Schwartz has a few choice pages on Reed that should disabuse anyone who still harbors illusions about him.)

One of the signal contributions of *Intellectuals and Assassins* may have been inadvertent: I mean its withering portrait of what has happened to the Nobel Prize for literature (and incidentally, for peace). The prize that once went to figures like T. S. Eliot and Thomas Mann now goes to talentless politically correct hucksters like Toni Morrison—or worse. Schwartz has several short chapters on some recent winners of that august prize, and it makes for sorry reading. Consider Rigoberta Menchu, the Guatemalan revolutionary who was awarded the Nobel Peace Prize in 1992. She was presented to the world as a symbol of "peace and reconciliation." In fact, Schwartz writes, her cause was not peace and reconciliation but guerrilla violence, "murder and subversion, as the Nordic snobs responsible for this ridiculous award know full well." Or consider Dario Fo, the 1997 Nobel laureate in literature. Jane Alexander, the outgoing head of the National Endowment for the Humanities, declared that Fo was "a very good choice. He's one of our greatest living playwrights." Schwartz comments: "Excuse me, our?" In fact, Dario Fo was and is an "anti-American extremist . . . an unrepentant hater of capitalism, religion, and common decency. In a century marked above all by the twin human tragedies of fascism and communism. Mr. Fo insists the real enemy is the supermarket."

It goes on and on. In 1998, the Nobel Prize for literature went to the Portuguese Communist José Saramago; in 1999, it went to the German novelist Gunter Grass, a vociferous supporter of the Sandinistas. Nor is the Nobel folly a recent phenomenon. In 1971, the prize went to Pablo Neruda, the Chilean poet, government functionary, and Stalinist who, among other things, helped an accomplice of Trotsky's assassin escape to Chile from Mexico after his first bungled attempt at murder. When Stalin died, Neruda wrote a eulogy (absent from the English edition of his works, but available in Spanish) in which we learn that

> To be men! That is the Stalinist law!
> ... We must learn from Stalin
> his sincere intensity
> his concrete clarity
> ... Stalin is the noon,
> the maturity of man and the peoples.
> Stalinists. Let us bear this title with pride.

There are a few heroes in *Intellectuals and Assassins*. But what Schwartz dilates most fully on are the rogues and blackguards that populated the Stalinist left. Taken as a whole, his book provides a portrait of "Stalinism and its seduction of intellectuals." It is a seduction that, even now, has not quite run its course. Schwartz concludes his book with the observation that "all things have a beginning and an end, and for the left, old as well as new, there is no further horizon. The time has come to sing a new song." One may hope that intellectuals find the courage and voice to sing those songs. It is the indisputable achievement of *Intellectuals and Assassins* to have shown how discordant the old melodies always were.

Chapter I:

INTELLECTUALS AND ASSASSINS

Intellectuals and Assassins:
Annals of Stalin's Killerati

In the latter half of the 1930s a gang of killers appeared in Western Europe whose accumulated crimes – considering their impact on history – are probably unequalled in the annals of murder. They were agents of the Soviet secret police – then called the N.K.V.D., later the K.G.B. – operating in a special "mobile unit" dedicated to terrorism.

The unit's existence became known through a series of sensational incidents 60 years ago – including the assassination in Switzerland in September 1937 of Ignace Reiss, an N.K.V.D. defector; the kidnapping from the streets of Paris of a White Russian general, Yevgeny Karlovich Miller, only weeks after Reiss's death; and, in the year 1938 alone, the terrorist slaying of Ukrainian nationalist leader Evhen Konovalets in Amsterdam, the kidnapping and torture-killing of Trotskyist functionary Rudolf Klement in Paris, and the murder in a Paris hospital of the son of Leon Trotsky, Lev Sedov.

Though centered in Paris, the group's tentacles reached into Spain, where an anti-Stalinist leftist, Andreu Nin, disappeared from police custody in June 1937. And in 1940 a leading member of the group, Soviet secret police general Naum Isakyevich Eitingon, known as "Leonid" Eitingon and generally as "Tom" in secret police communications, directed the assassination of Trotsky in Mexico.

The unit's activities involved a remarkable assortment of individuals, none of whom resemble the typical denizen of crime stories. Most of the key figures were intellectuals: poets, artists and psychiatrists. John J. Dziak, a historian who worked for the U.S. Defence Intelligence Agency, called attention to a nearly incredible chapter in the history of this team, one largely overlooked before him. In his book, *Chekisty: A History of the KGB*, Dziak reported that one of the group's key agents in the kidnapping of General Miller was none other than a close personal associate of Sigmund Freud and a pillar of the psychoanalytic movement, Dr. Max Eitingon, a relative of Gen. Naum Eitingon.

Further, there is convincing evidence that Dr. Max Eitingon was instrumental in preparing the 1937 secret trial in which the highest leaders of the Soviet Army, including the chief army commissar and eight generals, fell before the Stalinist execution machine. As the historian Robert Conquest established, to contrive evidence against the generals the special unit connived with Reinhard Heydrich of Hitler's intelligence service.

Freud's associate, Dr. Max Eitingon, was not the only well-known intellectual to be drawn into the work of the unit. Another of its members, Mordechai "Mark" Zborowski, a retired anthropologist and psychologist, died in 1991 in San Francisco. Yet another, Sergei Efron, was the husband of the Russian poet Marina Tsvetayeva. In his Mexican operation against Trotsky, Naum Eitingon secured the services of the painter David Alfaro Siqueiros, who led a massive armed attack on Trotsky's house in May 1940, three months before the successful assassination.

As documented in the memoirs of Gen. L. A. Sanchez Salazar, the chief Mexican police officer responsible for investigating the Trotsky case, the poet Pablo Neruda was suspended from his position with the Chilean diplomatic service for aiding the Eitingon network by providing Siqueiros with a visa that allowed him to escape from the Mexican authorities. The unit's tentacles extended as far as the group around the composer Igor Stravinsky and the Prague Linguistic Circle including the Russian formalist critic and linguist Roman Jakobson.

How can we believe such things of such people? Yet the evidence in the matter has never been disproven, and nearly all of it has been in print for some time. Aside from Dziak, the French historian Pierre Broué, the American Sovietologist Natalie Grant, and others extensively researched the Eitingon-Efron-Zborowski active group for "special tasks" and its relationship with the N.K.V.D. centre in Moscow. Since the fall of Soviet Communism, a series of memoirs and documentary releases have supported disclosures that in many cases were made long before.

Indeed, one of the great ironies of post-Communist historiography is that very little of the material released from Soviet archives since 1991 tells us anything really new. Perhaps the most just comment on the whole series of killings, which I have come to call "Stalin's Western Assault," was delivered in 1999, when Christopher Andrew and Vasili Mitrokhin commented, in *The Mitrokhin Archive*, "many admirable studies of the Stalin era fail to mention the relentless secret pursuit of 'enemies of the people' in Western Europe." Unfortunately, a number of cases remain unelucidated, including some in the Western Hemisphere: the disappearance in New York in 1938 of the Communist leader Juliet Stuart Poyntz and the assassination five years later of the Italian-American labour leader Carlo Tresca, the mysterious death in 1942 of the Communist photographer, Tina Modotti, in Mexico City, and the death in the same town of the German anti-Stalinist Otto Rühle.

The earliest sign of the existence of the special unit seems to be the appearance of a young Russian, Lev Narvich, at the headquarters of the dissident Marxist party, the Partit Obrer d'Unificació Marxista (P.O.U.M.), in Barcelona early in 1937. Narvich, claiming to be a critic of Soviet policies in Spain, obtained interviews with Andreu Nin, a well-known Catalan literary figure and main leader of the P.O.U.M. Narvich, who was also a photographer, insisted on taking pictures of the party leaders and others at the headquarters. On June 16, thanks to Soviet pressure on the Spanish Republican Government, the leaders of the P.O.U.M., Nin included, were arrested and charged with high treason.

Nin disappeared within days and was never seen again. By the 1980s, even the leaders of the Communist Party in Spain admitted that Nin was murdered on Stalin's orders; he was killed within days of his disappearance. Narvich's photographs were used to identify foreign P.O.U.M. sympathizers. George Orwell, who was in Barcelona soon after the arrests but then fled Spain in fear of arrest himself, may have escaped precisely because he was not photographed by Narvich. Orwell was, in any event, marked for possible removal to Russia and certain execution if he was caught.

In Paris Narvich had been a member of the Union for Repatriation of Russians Abroad, a Soviet-controlled front organization aimed at infiltrating the exiled community of White Russians. Also connected with this organization were four more members of the special unit – Gen. Nikolai Vasilyevich Skoblin, his wife Nadyezhda Plevitskaya, Dr. Max Eitingon and Sergei Efron – who were involved in the murder of Ignace Reiss and the disappearance of General Miller. Ignace Reiss, born Ignacy Porecki in Polish Galicia, was a high officer in Soviet military intelligence operating in Switzerland. The network he set up included an American, a close friend of Alger Hiss, Noel Field, who lived in Hungary beginning in the late 1940's. In her book, *Red Pawn: The Story of Noel Field*, Flora Lewis, a columnist for *The New York Times*, convincingly argued that Field was involved in the activities with which Hiss was charged by Whittaker Chambers. Further corroboration of espionage activities of Field and Hiss comes from the Venona papers, a set of decrypted secret Soviet communications from the early 1940s, which were released to the public by the U.S. authorities in the late 1990s.

Early in 1937, Reiss, when he learned of the imminent attack on the P.O.U.M. and Nin, defected from the N.K.V.D. and, in a blistering letter addressed to Stalin, proclaimed his solidarity with the Trotskyists. He then went underground. He was tracked down near Lausanne, Switzerland, and assassinated on September 4, 1937. An accomplice of the murderers was caught by the Swiss police, and the conspiracy began to unravel.

On September 22, the news of the kidnapping of General Miller swept Paris. Miller had left a letter behind, stating that he was to meet with another White Russian, Gen. Nikolai Vasilyevich Skoblin. Working with the Swiss, the French police discovered that someone named Vadim Kondratiev, who was involved with Efron in the murder of Reiss, was a subordinate and friend of Skoblin. Skoblin, who had served as the courier between Reinhard Heydrich and the N.K.V.D., was the real prize, and he disappeared immediately. His wife, Nadyezhda Plevitskaya, a famous Russian folk singer, was arrested and sentenced by a French court for complicity in the kidnapping of Miller. She died in a French prison during World War II. It was through the Skoblin-Plevitskaya case that the revelations about Freud's colleague, Dr. Eitingon, were made.

Just about the time Narvich appeared in Barcelona, Skoblin approached Heydrich, head of the Nazi security service, or Sicherheitsdienst (S.D). Skoblin communicated with the Germans about a supposed conspiracy between the German General Staff and the Soviet generals who were later to be condemned in the secret trial. Heydrich manufactured documents supporting the claim and these were passed on to Stalin. The Soviet generals were tried and executed in June 1937, beginning the vast purge of officers that would leave the army virtually leaderless when Hitler invaded the Soviet Union in 1941. The details of this operation were first outlined by a Soviet defector, Walter Krivitsky, who explained that Gen. Miller had been kidnapped because he knew too much about the forging of "evidence" in the case.

In his book, Dziak concluded that Dr. Max Eitingon recruited Skoblin and Plevitskaya into the special unit. That charge is supported by other historians as well as by documents from the Plevitskaya trial. At the time of the kidnapping of General Miller, Dr. Eitingon had decamped for Palestine, where he had previously established a psychoanalytic institute. The dissident Soviet historians Vitaly Rapoport and Yuri Alexeev declared flatly in their book, *High Treason*, that Dr. Eitingon, serving his relative Naum, was the control agent for Skoblin and Plevitskaya. Plevitskaya described him at her trial as her financial angel.

One might have thought that the somewhat retiring psychoanalyst, the only member of the Freud inner circle or "secret seven" never to have written extensively for the analytical public, would have done his best to steer clear of the Plevitskaya proceeding, the most sensational trial of its time in France. In addition, Dr. Eitingon was a Jew, and the social stratum in which Skoblin and Plevitskaya were best known was notoriously anti-Semitic. But in a series of strange contretemps, Dr. Eitingon attempted to assist Plevitskaya. From Palestine, he sent Princess Marie Bonaparte, another prominent member of the psychoanalytic movement, to the Paris tribunal, in a fruitless attempt to offer character testimony in defence of the Russian singer. The presence of Princess Bonaparte in the courtroom generated newspaper headlines, but she was barred from appearing as a witness. Dr. Eitingon did not, however, go to Paris himself. Even more peculiarly, he wrote evasive letters to the aging Freud – his last, in fact, to the master – in which he tried to dismiss "the affair of the Russian singer" as an expression of petit bourgeois French stupidity.

The key to the entire Eitingon matter doubtless lies in the source of his income as well as that of the psychoanalytic movement in general. Max Eitingon lived off the profits of a fur company, the Eitingon-Schild, which had been established in Russia long before the Revolution, and which maintained branches throughout Europe as well as in America. After the Bolshevik takeover, Eitingon-Schild was granted a monopoly for the sale of Russian furs abroad, a major source of hard currency for the struggling Soviet regime. Dr. Max Eitingon used his share of the family wealth to pay for the Berlin Psychoanalytic Institute and the Psychanalytischer Verlag, the official publishing house of the Freudian movement. But after 1917 this money came through Soviet hands, as well.

Dr. Eitingon complained in the 1930s that he had to reduce his subsidy to the Verlag because of financial losses incurred by the company during the worldwide depression, but it is not outside the realm of possibility that the Stalin regime, while agreeable to Eitingon money being used to finance spying, was no longer willing to see it spent on psychoanalysis. Some later authors have questioned whether the Stalin regime would have continued using a Freudian as a spy considering its ideological objections to Freud's theory. But that is an absurd line of argument: Stalinist agents included Nazis and homosexuals, as well as the anti-Semitic friends of Stravinsky, even though the N.K.V.D. certainly would not have tolerated Nazism, homosexuality, or Stravinsky's music for internal consumption in the U.S.S.R. That Alger Hiss, a leading figure in the Rooseveltian New Deal, spied for Stalin should not be taken to suggest that Stalin intended to introduce the New Deal in the Soviet Union. Indeed, notwithstanding Stalinist opposition to psychoanalysis as a theory, psychiatrists, with their access to the secrets of the elite, would have made spectacular spies.

In any event, Dr. Max Eitingon had been under suspicion, by many who observed him, for a long time. An early story published in English by the young Russian émigré writer Vladimir Nabokov, "The Assistant Producer," is a recounting of the Skoblin-Plevitskaya affair, in which Eitingon appears under a pseudonym, as a sinister presence. Nabokov had lived in Berlin, where Dr. Eitingon resided before Hitler came to power, and knew whereof he spoke.

Trotsky's son, Lev Sedov, died on February 16, 1938, following an appendicitis operation in a Paris hospital run by Russians associated with the Union for Repatriation. But he did not die as a result of the surgery. Another leading agent in his death was Mordechai "Mark" Zborowski, then an anthropology student and Trotskyist activist. Zborowski, a former member of the Union for Repatriation, managed to win the confidence of Sedov so completely that Sedov trusted Zborowski to receive and open his mail.

Zborowski admitted to Congressional investigators that he brought Sedov to that hospital so the special unit could kidnap him, but he claimed he did not know they intended to kill him. However, a French medical report sustains the suspicion that Sedov was murdered in the hospital bed. Zborowski later told a high official in the American Central Intelligence Agency that he had killed Sedov with a poisoned orange, the remains of which appear in the medical report. Zborowski had previously played an informant's role in leading the special unit to Ignace Reiss's hiding place in Switzerland. In a less horrifying episode, he supervised the N.K.V.D. theft of a section of Trotsky's archives, held in Paris at a historical institute.

As noted, the special "mobile unit" had other kills to its credit as well, including that of one of Trotsky's secretaries, Erwin Wolf, who disappeared in Spain, and Rudolf Klement, a Trotskyist leader whose decapitated corpse was found in the Seine. No documents have been released from the Soviet archives on these cases; almost nothing can be confirmed about their fates. To established historians, they are of little or no consequence: minor figures from a forgotten movement, who happened to die horribly, as young and innocent men, for their ideals. Few remember them, fewer speak about them, even fewer would advocate for them. Perhaps they, like others, might have gone on to careers as leading intellectuals, to honour and respect, even to an anti-Communist outlook. Such opportunities were denied them; they had chosen unwisely, in history's cruel game, and they paid for it with their obscure, unknowable, but worthy lives. Perhaps they were even heroes, although nearly anonymously.

Sergei Efron and his wife, Marina Tsvetayeva, fled France in the wake of the Reiss and Miller affairs. Efron had pretended for 20 years that he too was an anti-Communist White Russian. But his wife followed him back to Russia, where he was purged from the N.K.V.D. and executed. She committed suicide.

Zborowski, who had come to the United States, was exposed in the 1950s as having worked for the K.G.B. In turn, he exposed a network of K.G.B. agents, and, after serving a sentence for perjury in connection with the various investigations of him, he returned to his profession as a medical anthropologist and had an honoured career. Until

15

his retirement in 1984, he was the director of the Pain Centre at Mount Zion Hospital in San Francisco. His role in the events I have been describing is a subject for much commentary by historians, among them Isaac Deutscher in *The Prophet Outcast: Trotsky 1929-1940*.

Now, who were the Eitingons? Naum Eitingon was considered the K.G.B.'s outstanding expert in operations against Russian anti-Communist exiles, as well as Trotskyists, and he used as a cover the business operations for the Soviet fur trust that benefited from the Eitingon-Schild enterprise. Gen. Eitingon turned up in Mexico, exploiting the identities and wealth of his relatives, and there directed the killing of Leon Trotsky, using as his agent Raimon Mercader, the son of a woman with whom he had an affair. But his biography is clouded by the continuing secrecy of his employers, the Soviet secret police, and their post-Communist successors. Certain memoirists, including his former colleague in "special tasks," Pavel A. Sudoplatov, seem to disclose a great deal about him, but much that appears in such works is defective on known and established details, particularly about the Trotsky assassination, which has been very thoroughly documented. Until Western historians are granted full and unrestricted access to Soviet biographical information on him, much about Naum Eitingon will remain unconfirmed.

About his relative, Dr. Max Eitingon, by contrast, we know a great deal. Born in 1881, Max Eitingon had been analysed by Freud, and he joined "the secret seven," the committee set up to defend the psychoanalytic movement from public, and, especially, anti-Semitic attacks. The committee included Freud, his biographer Ernest Jones, Otto Rank, Karl Abraham, Sandor Ferenczi, Hanns Sachs and Max Eitingon. A famous photograph of the seven, which hung in Freud's waiting room and which has been widely reproduced, shows Dr. Eitingon in the second row, behind Freud and between Abraham and Jones. He is somewhat short, bald, with piercing eyes.

In the late 1930s, Dr. Eitingon was Freud's last close confidante from among "the secret seven." Abraham was dead, Ferenczi and Rank were deeply alienated from the master, and Sachs and Jones were unsuited to the role. Anna Freud even fell in love with him at one time. As early as 1922, Freud told him: "I suggest we continue our relationship, which has developed from friendship to sonship, until the end of my days."

Dr. Max Eitingon was not an impressive figure. Paul Roazen, in his book *Freud and His Followers,* says "it is hard to say much about Eitingon, since he was not a good teacher or speaker (he had a stammer), and he wrote next to nothing." After he died in Jerusalem in 1943, Hanns Sachs, a fellow member of "the secret seven" wrote: "Max Eitingon played an outstanding, unforgettable role in the history of the psychoanalytic movement although his name is not connected with the development of any special part of psychoanalytic theory."

We will probably never know how Dr. Eitingon felt about his and his relative's N.K.V.D. activities. It may be argued that his own participation, over all, must have been slight, although without his involvement as the link to Skoblin the liquidation of the Soviet generals might not have been carried out so easily. And, not to put too fine a point on it, it is not pleasant to imagine an associate of Freud in league with a henchman of Heydrich. Yet that detail is unarguable: Dr. Eitingon, the companion of Freud, sent his friend Princess Marie Bonaparte to Paris to succour Plevitskaya, the wife of Skoblin, who conspired with Heydrich. As the later phrase would have it, between Dr. Eitingon and Heydrich there were only two degrees of separation at most.

In the photograph of the "secret committee" Dr. Eitingon appears mild-mannered, kindly, benign. In this he resembles many of the other figures whose names appear in this story. He was an intellectual, not a thug, a man of medicine, not a party militant. But Siqueiros and Neruda, on whose services Naum Eitingon drew in the murder of Trotsky in Mexico, were, respectively, a painter and a poet. Efron was the husband of one of the most sensitive poets of this century. And Zborowski gained fame as a researcher on pain.

Could the case of Dr. Eitingon be merely an extreme example of what the journalist and historian Paul Johnson has called "the heartlessness of intellectuals?" Or might the psychoanalyst have been no more than the victim, as was Tsvetayeva, of loyalty to a family relationship? Dziak and others believe that Dr. Eitingon's responsibility in the Skoblin affair was more than superficial, but what can we say about the doctor's intent? Perhaps nothing. Certainly, unlike Tsvetayeva, Krivitsky, Siqueiros and Neruda, Dr. Eitingon left no plea or testament that would reveal his state of mind, aside from his last letter to Freud, in which he attempted to exculpate Plevitskaya. His relative Naum also stands mute before history, although we know that after Stalin's death he was imprisoned for some time in the Soviet Union. A similar fate might very well have befallen Zborowski had he heeded the Russians' many demands for his return to the Soviet Union before his public unmasking in the United States.

If there is a moral to be drawn from this tale, it must be something along the following lines: When Stalin's men sought agents for the most depraved and most criminal tasks, they found them not only among brutes of the underworld, but among sensitive and cultivated people in the highest levels of intellectual society – poets and psychiatrists who became conspirators and spies.

– The New York Times Book Review, January 24, 1988

Marina Tsvetayeva:
The Poetess and the Spy
(With Leon Aron)

Marina Tsvetayeva, born in 1892, hanged herself in 1941 and was buried in an unmarked grave. She was one of the most gifted Russian writers of all time. Between her glorious, fulfilled youth and her terrible fate she "entered the whirlwind" of revolution and counter-revolution. She lent her voice to the anti-Communist White Russian movement and yet found her reputation sullied by an association with the terror operations of Stalin's secret police, then known as the N.K.V.D.

As a teenager, Marina Tsvetayeva gained fame for her remarkable poetic gifts. At the same time she became involved with a man named Sergei Efron. He was a writer of some talent linked with the terrorist People's Will movement of tsarist times.

With the coming of the revolution, Efron joined the anti-Bolshevik armies. Tsvetayeva returned to Moscow, intending at first to join him; but she was forced to stay in the Red zone. She was respected as a poet by the Bolshevik intellectuals, although Efron's service on the other side was well known. She professed to hate the Communists and wrote many poems in honour of the White soldiery. But she also worked briefly for the Bolshevik government, under, of all people, Stalin.

In 1921, while she was still in Moscow, Tsvetayeva received news that Efron had survived the civil war and emigrated to Czechoslovakia. Marina immediately joined him.

In the late 1920s Efron began to express pro-Soviet sympathies. These became so pronounced as to make Tsvetayeva an object of suspicion in the Russian exile community in Paris. Eventually, Efron became involved with a Russian-speaking Paris group operating as a front for the N.K.V.D., the Union for Repatriation of Russians Abroad.

The political life of the Efron family seems to have proceeded at a rather lazy pace until the assassination in Switzerland – on September 4, 1937, at the height of the Soviet purges – of a middle aged man bearing a passport identifying him as a Czech citizen named Hans Eberhard.

Eberhard's real name was Ignacy Porecki. He was also known as Ignace Reiss, and was a senior official of Stalin's secret police. A veteran of the Communist International or Comintern, as well as Red Army Intelligence (G.R.U.), he had played a crucial role in Soviet espionage in the West.

Ten weeks before his death, Reiss had begun a protest against the purges in the U.S.S.R., which had just decapitated the Red armed forces, and which Stalin had ordered extended to Republican Spain, in the middle of its civil war. Reiss broke with Stalin in a thundering letter, returned his decorations, proclaimed his solidarity with the exiled Leon Trotsky, and warned against an extension of the N.K.V.D. into the West, specifically, the Spanish Republic. His liquidation came almost immediately.

The Reiss murder was a central event in the history of Soviet intelligence operations, leading to more deaths and involving personnel also assigned to the murder of Trotsky. A complicated trail led the Swiss police, seeking Reiss's killers, to France. With the cooperation of the French police, the centre of the terrorist group was located in Paris, in the office of the Union for Repatriation of Russians Abroad and in the person of Efron.

Efron escaped the police net and returned to the U.S.S.R. via Republican Spain, but the scandal alienated many Russian exiles from Tsvetayeva, including the novelist Vladimir Nabokov, who agreed with the widespread belief that she was a knowing and deceitful Soviet agent. To make matters worse, Efron's group was also connected with a conspiracy to murder Trotsky's son, Lev Sedov, and to the sensational kidnapping of White Russian general Yevgeny Karlovich Miller. The Reiss, Sedov, and Miller cases have become subjects for academic commentators on Tsvetayeva's work. The single question with which all have wrestled centres on how much she knew about Efron's activities.

Efron had fled to the U.S.S.R. Her daughter Ariadne having preceded him, Tsvetayeva herself, with her son Grigory, nicknamed Mur, returned to her homeland. For some time she and Efron enjoyed the patronage of the N.K.V.D. But Efron's performance in the Reiss case had not been brilliant. He was soon purged and executed. Marina committed suicide in 1941, after the German invasion of Russia forced her evacuation to the interior of the country. Desperate, she hanged herself.

The mystery has long remained: how much did she know? The question may never be answered in full. But a key document, long considered lost by specialists, lies in the archives of the Hoover Institution in California: the record of the French police interrogation of the poetess. It does not provide a full picture of her state of mind at the time of Reiss's murder, but it should help correct many inaccuracies and fantasies, including tales of hysterical recitations of verse to the French detectives.

The document shows that Tsvetayeva said her husband had left France to volunteer in the Spanish Republican Army. She also said she had no idea what he did when he occasionally left Paris, and never asked him about his business.

These we believe to be lies formulated by Tsvetayeva to protect her husband. Efron was a weak individual, extremely dependent on Tsvetayeva with no business or income apart from what he received from her and from the N.K.V.D. She must have known he was headed "home," to the U.S.S.R., where she soon followed him.

Throughout their relationship Marina had betrayed Sergei Efron, pursuing numerous affairs. But at the end she remained loyal to him in the face of the police.

Yet we still find such a verdict incomplete. In this late act of her drama, Marina Tsvetayeva accomplished not an act of baseness, but of nobility. She protected the man to whom she had sworn her life. The Stalinists created a morality that sought to punish spouses and offspring for their relatives' actions. But it is not in the tradition of Western law to condemn a wife for her refusal to bear witness against her husband. That her courage and sacrifice would be crushed and deformed by the evil of Stalinism seems to have been, as in so many other cases, an inevitability.

– Arguments and Facts International, 1989

Anna Akhmatova:
A Stark Voice Tempered by Soviet Tragedy

(Author's note: Some readers may consider it inappropriate to include the pre-sent article, and the following one on Osip Mandelshtam, in tandem with stud-ies of Stalinist intellectuals and of the fate of Marina Tsvetayeva. Akhmatova and Mandelshtam were never Stalinists; they were among the most prominent victims of Stalin. However, because they are always grouped with Tsvetayeva (and Boris Pasternak) among the greatest Russian poets of the 20th century, it seems justifiable to join them to Tsvetayeva, if only as counter-examples, show-ing that not all Russian intellectuals were susceptible to the contagion.)

Russian novelists are better known in the West than Russian poets, but the great figures of modern Russian poetry are finding a growing readership outside the Slavic world. Anna Akhmatova was a leading 20th-century Russian poet whose life was also emblematic of the cultural devastation of the Soviet era. Her poetry, with its clarity and sharp imagery, contributed to the modernist transformation of Russian literature. She published five splendid collections of verse during the late tsarist period and the first postrevolutionary decade – between 1912 and 1921 – but all of it was eventually suppressed, and she suffered great personal tragedy at the hands of the Soviet state. Her story is given a full and conscientious treatment in Roberta Reeder's massive new biography, *Anna Akhmatova: Poet and Prophet.*

Akhmatova was born Anna Gorenko near Odessa in Ukraine. Her father was a naval engineer who was granted noble status for his ser-vice to the czar. In 1910 she moved to St. Petersburg, where her first collection, *Evening,* was soon published.

This was the close of Russia's "Silver Age," a period that had featured great cultural as well as economic development in Russia. In literature, the period was dominated by an ornate and rhetorically heavy symbol-ist style, of which the best-known exponent remains Alexander Blok. By

21

contrast, Akhmatova's poetic line was clean, direct and uncluttered.

This was, as they say, no accident. Two years before *Evening* appeared, Akhmatova had married a fellow poet, Nikolai Gumilyov, and soon after she met Osip Mandelshtam, certainly the greatest Russian poet of this century. The three together led a new poetic movement, which they called acmeism. In its emphasis on precision and clarity, acmeism amounted to a renunciation of the symbolist vogue. Its claims were similar to those of Ezra Pound's imagism in England, although the Russian movement retained certain passionate and mystical elements.

The coming of World War I and the 1917 Russian Revolution transformed all their lives. Gumilyov was executed by the Soviet authorities for counterrevolutionary activities. Akhmatova, who had amicably divorced Gumilyov in 1918 after growing weary of his unlimited pursuit of other women, was left with their son, Lev, who was in turn arrested and imprisoned in 1933 on a charge of anti-Soviet agitation.

A year later Mandelshtam – who had come to be Akhmatova's most intimate poetic colleague after Gumilyov – was arrested because of a poem that alluded to Stalin's brutality. (Akhmatova was in fact present in Mandelshtam's apartment during the arrest.) He died in a prison camp a few years later.

The Stalinist assault on Akhmatova's life did not end there. Lev Gumilyov was arrested again in 1938. He refused to confess to false charges and so was interrogated cruelly for eight months, transferred from prison to a labour camp and eventually sent to Siberia.

The loss of Gumilyov and of Mandelshtam, as well as the persecution of her son, led Akhmatova to compose the haunting poetic cycle "Requiem," justly famous for its extraordinarily beautiful language and its ghastly concrete images:

> Quietly flows the quiet Don,
> Yellow moon slips into a home.
> He slips in with cap askew,
> He sees a shadow, yellow moon.
>
> This woman is ill,
> This woman is alone,
> Husband in the grave, son in prison,
> Say a prayer for me.

Lev Gumilyov was released during World War II and allowed to fight in the Soviet army. Akhmatova, despite her experiences, retained a patriotic loyalty to Russia and supported the Soviet Union unstintingly in its war with Nazi Germany, even writing an unforgettable poem, "Courage," that became a kind of soldier's anthem.

Even so, her modernist poetry was attacked by Stalin's henchmen soon after the war ended – for its "hopelessness, mysticism and eroticism" – and she was expelled from the Union of Soviet Writers. It was not until the Soviet "thaw" of the late 1950s that she was allowed to republish her work. In 1965 she brought out her first new collection since 1940. She died a year later.

If there is a moral to the Akhmatova story, it is a simple and even obvious one: that art and intellect can triumph over tyranny. The horrors of communism did not destroy Akhmatova, personally or poetically, but rather lifted her to extraordinary heights of achievement.

Ms. Reeder is a leading academic expert on Akhmatova. Like many other American academic products, this book stands less as an original biographical work than as a kind of anthology of memoirs, citations, critical appreciations and other materials from previously printed sources.

Nevertheless, the noble and nightmarish epic of Anna Akhmatova makes this book very much worth reading.

–The Wall Street Journal, February 6, 1995

Osip Mandelshtam:
Reclaiming a Writer, Doubter, Outsider and Martyr

The tragedy and achievement of the Russian poet Osip Mandelshtam now draws a wide reading public in his native Russian language, two decades after he and his work came to the attention of Western readers. This is, of course, not a paradox; although Mandelshtam was an extraordinarily talented and important modern poet, his life was snuffed out by Stalinism in 1939 and knowledge of his verses was suppressed during the remaining 50 years of Soviet communism.

Mandelshtam was originally rescued from this deliberately imposed oblivion thanks to his widow, Nadezhda Mandelshtam, who long outlived him and who produced a striking memoir of their short life together, *Hope Against Hope*. That book became a classic of anti-Stalinist dissidence, circulated in the 1960s by the now dimly remembered medium of *samizdat*, or self-publishing by typewriter.

Osip Emilievich Mandelshtam was born in 1891 in Warsaw to a non-observant Jewish family that soon moved to St. Petersburg. As a young man he underwent an Orthodox Christian conversion, so as to attend a decent school. He was a revolutionary early on, but by the coming of the Russian Revolution in 1917 his work was almost entirely lyrical, mystical, amorous, and modernist, with virtually no sign of overt political concerns.

The year 1922 saw publication outside Russia of his collection *Tristia*, its titled borrowed from Ovid ("The Sorrows"). That book is, for the present writer, one of the purest and most completed collections of verse ever assembled. It also includes several poems about the Revolution that are so memorable in their chilling impact that they may stand as the single most important literary product of that terrible human disaster.

"Brothers, let's drink to the twilight of freedom", he wrote in one poem, comparing the revolutionary triumph to the militarisation of birds, whose flight has blocked the sun. And yet, the poem ends in a note of bitter, obviously illusory optimism:

> In hell's frozen waters we will tell ourselves
> This Earth we won was worth ten heavens.

Remarkably enough, as Clare Cavanagh, an associate professor of Slavic languages at the University of Wisconsin, points out in *Osip Mandelstam and the Modernist Creation of Tradition*, these prophetic words were put into print in the *Red Militiaman*, an organ of the Bolshevik regime, opposite an article hailing the brutal suppression of an anti-communist sailors' revolt at the fortress of Kronstadt. And these lines by no means offered his only dazzling insight into Russia's deadly future. In another poem from the same collection, he spoke of St. Petersburg as a mystical city, Petropolis, and of the death of its spiritual double or "brother" foretold by the appearance of a wandering star in the skies.

In what may be his most beautiful and affecting poem, also from *Tristia*, he wrote:

In Petersburg we will meet again
As if we left the sun buried there
And the blessed word that has no sense
We will speak as if for the very first time.

That poem's prophecy was fulfilled, when, after communism's fall, Russians again came together in that city, which regained its original name, changed at the time the poem was written to Petrograd, and then to Leningrad. They pronounced anew the "senseless" words they had lost: freedom, love, even the religious word "blessed" (*blazhyen-noye*, which appears in the Slavonic Christian liturgy.)

Mandelshtam died in 1939 in the GuLag, of a heart attack. His final drama began in 1934, with his composition of a poem alluding to the massacres wrought by the unnamed but obviously intended Stalin, evoking the dictator as "the Kremlin mountaineer," and a Caucasian tribesman, and finally saying that the "broad-chested" ruler enjoyed every death, as if eating raspberry jam.

"This is not a literary fact but an act of suicide," Boris Pasternak said of that work. Pasternak knew whereof he spoke. Mandelshtam had read the poem in question at a party in Pasternak's house, and after Mandelshtam's arrest Pasternak received a telephone call from Stalin himself, questioning him about Mandelshtam. That encounter, one of the most famous in Russian intellectual history, ended inconclusively for Pasternak, but for Mandelshtam a terrible void had opened up.

Soon Mandelshtam was undergoing brutal interrogations by the secret police, in which he answered the demands for an explanation of his lines on Stalin by saying simply, "I hate fascism." Such candour typically led to more beatings. However, he was not immediately executed or even deported to the Siberian camps. At first he was sent into internal exile in a city away from Moscow. He was said to have benefited from the protection of "right wing" Communist ideologist Nikolai Bukharin, a favourite of Lenin, until Bukharin in turn fell before the Stalinist scythe. Mandelshtam, then, was well and truly lost. He was sent to the most remote and inhospitable region of the GuLag, beyond the Arctic Circle and close to the Pacific Ocean, where he died.

Mandelshtam's relation with language was mystical, sensuous, and even one might say, rather kabbalistic as he made his way forward, a

Jew plunged into Christian culture. This sensitivity drew him to both Hebrew and Christian tradition, even to a certain classicism, but his involvement with language made him both traditional and modern, rather than modernism transforming his language. Unlike Pound and Eliot, he created modernism more then he was created by it.

Ms. Cavanagh writes at length on "Jewish" elements in Mandelshtam's work, citing the anti-Semitic claims of Richard Wagner's disciples, who declared that Jews could only "borrow" German and other languages, and that in their language a Jewish "inner voice" must inevitably lurk. In reality, although Mandelshtam's diction was, as Ms. Cavanagh observes, marked by "foreign, unauthorized, chaotic speech that set him apart" from other Russian writers, it is an obnoxious cliché to associate such a stylistic pattern in some psychological way with Jewishness.

While Mandelshtam, the gifted writer, doubter, "outsider," and martyr represented a common Jewish type in our time, his language was unique and cannot be redacted as a mix of Jewish and other cultures. Indeed, his discourse seems so quintessentially Slavic to some that today's Russian anti-Semites have been known to claim him as an authentic Orthodox Christian, with no Jewish antecedents!

There is much to say about Mandelshtam as a modernist icon, but a work such as Ms. Cavanagh's, while undoubtedly useful for scholars, will hardly win Mandelshtam the wider English-reading audience he deserves, not only for the exceptional courage of his anti-Stalinism but, above all, for the melody and depth of his verse.

–Forward (New York), March 24, 1995

* * * * *

Chapter II:

THE POST-SOVIET TRANSITION

Sombre Thoughts in San Francisco

The Armenian national flag is a sombre affair, a horizontal tricolour of red, blue, and orange. It reminds one of sunset over a long, dusty road; of ancient rivers, of blood. When Soviet president Mikhail Gorbachev arrived in San Francisco the evening of June 3, 1990, he was greeted by dozens of Armenian banners waving in the foggy dark. Outraged by the killing of nationalist militants in Soviet Armenia, California's half-million Armenian community – the largest in the Armenian diaspora – turned out a large delegation to protest the president's visit.

California governor George Deukmejian, an Armenian as well as a conservative Republican with considerable support from the local business community, was waiting at the Soviet consular residence to greet Gorbachev – and to bring up the economic boycott that has been declared by the Soviet government against Armenia. It was there, with Deukmejian waiting on the pavement, that Gorbachev made the second major blunder of his trip. Pleading lack of time, he left Deukmejian in the courtyard, although presenting the California governor with a medal for aid to Armenian earthquake victims.

The next day, once again, a substantial encounter with Deukmejian was avoided. As Gorbachev arrived at San Francisco's Fairmont Hotel for an afternoon banquet, his limousine entered the parking lot, where the gate swung shut just ahead of Deukmejian's vehicle.

The latter snub, in which a visiting Soviet dignitary humiliated the governor of an American state on the latter's own ground, seemed to sum up the dominant style of Soviet politics over many decades, even under Gorbachev.

As noted, however, these were not the first such missteps. An error of much greater importance came during his press conference just days before in Washington, when Gorbachev declared his government might block further emigration of Jews unless the U.S. were to pressure Israel to ensure they would not be settled in the occupied territories. In the U.S., where Jewish opinion is so influential, this was a statement of no small consequences. It was reported some time later that Soviet foreign minister Eduard Shevardnadze had assured U.S. secretary of state James Baker that no disruption in orderly emigration should be anticipated.

The 150 or so American business leaders who gathered at a banquet in San Francisco to welcome the Soviet president were wary. Gorbachev urged those present to commit early to investment in the U.S.S.R., arguing that those who acted boldly would reap profits. "Those who cooperate with us now will see many more opportunities for further cooperation, but those who stay on the sidelines will remain there – and I think that will be fair," Gorbachev declared.

He insisted, "we are now watching – watching those who are risking something and who are willing to cooperate at this time and watching those who stand on the sidelines." He promised that rouble convertibility, a major problem for Western business, would soon be introduced, but offered no details.

Business people at the luncheon applauded Gorbachev, but most said they had come more out of a desire to show hospitality than out of interest in the Soviet economy. "This is an event, not a relationship builder," commented one executive. Another said, "Our attendance is just a civic expression of welcome." Indeed, the whole visit seemed to have provided little more than an opportunity for an orgy of Californian narcissism.

If there was anything for Gorbachev to celebrate in his San Francisco visit, it was his meeting with Roh Tae Woo, president of South Korea. The contact represented an undeniable breakthrough in Soviet Pacific relations. Gorbachev alluded to the importance of this event by quoting the 19th century Russian liberal Aleksandr Herzen, who described the Pacific Basin as a "future Mediterranean."

Such comments were appropriate, for the Roh meeting curiously skewed Gorbachev's performance at this summit. In the final reckoning of things, he accomplished more on his side trip to the U.S. West Coast than in his talks with president George Bush.

But Gorbachev might have been better served had he recalled another quote from Herzen. The following comment appears in the 1855 work *From the Other Shore:*

28

"The revolution of Peter the Great replaced the obsolete squirearchy of Russia – with a European bureaucracy; everything that could be copied from the Swedish and German laws, everything that could be taken over from the free municipalities of Holland into our half communal, half absolutist country, was taken over. But the unwritten, the moral check on power, the instinctive recognition of the rights of man, of the rights of thought, of truth, could not be and were not imported."

–Arguments and Facts International, September 1990

"India of the North"

At the beginning of the process of reform in the Soviet Union, late in 1987, former U.S. defence secretary Donald H. Rumsfeld wrote, "Tensions within the Soviet system make it appear that some kind of reversion to a more normal civic existence… could conceivably take place. And something like that is what Gorbachev seems to have promised the world."

However, Rumsfeld at that time also issued a warning against excessive optimism. He noted, "We hail Gorbachev while forgetting the lessons of Lenin and Khrushchev, Stalin and Brezhnev. Vladimir Voinovich, in analysing glasnost (Gorbachev's policy of 'candour' in public affairs – author's note), has cited an appropriate precedent even further back, warning of the parallel between Gorbachev and tsar Aleksandr II, who ruled in the middle of the 19th century. 'Only when it became clear that certain basic reforms… could no longer be avoided, were these reforms decreed.'" Rumsfeld, still citing Voinovich, then pointed out that the liberalization of Aleksandr II gave way to terror, a rightist reaction, and eventually, the disaster of 1917.

Thus, Gorbachev is not the first Russian or Soviet leader to preach reform once it has become unavoidable. His most famous predecessor on this road might be Lenin himself, founder of the Soviet state, who adopted the New Economic Policy or N.E.P., including restoration of private enterprise, in order to prolong the overall rule of the Communist Party.

29

Indeed, Stalin, to prevent a complete collapse of his regime during the Second World War, was compelled to re-establish religious worship in the Soviet Union, and dropped typical Communist propaganda slogans, ordering a return to Russian nationalism.

In both cases, what appeared to be healthy trends, acclaimed by sympathizers and even some opponents of Communism, were paired with equally negative actions or reversed once the immediate crisis was past. By 1930, private and foreign capital were once again repressed in Russia. Within a year of war's end in 1945, writers and others who had rallied to defend Russian culture from Nazi aggression were subjected to incredible abuse, and a new wave of Stalinist purges began.

Sadly, Rumsfeld's warning must now be seen as a timely one. Certainly, whether his prediction turns out to be correct in the long run, the majority of American policy and business leaders no longer profess the enthusiastic hopes and plans about Soviet-Western cooperation and the transformation of the Soviet system that were in vogue even a year ago.

For most informed Americans, the probable outcome for Russia appears bleaker than ever. In the place of an inefficient socialism that encouraged scarcity, there has appeared a wholesale poverty... The past threat of Soviet revolutionary expansionism has been replaced by the spectre of wholesale ethnic warfare. With the fall of the party bureaucracy has come the emergence of a powerful Soviet mafia.

The picture of Russia's future held by American leaders increasingly resembles an "India of the North:" a country that may achieve a partial or superficial democratisation, but which is simply too handicapped by cultural factors to attain the stability and prosperity for which it hopes. With the political caste system and hypertrophied state structure remaining in place, such a power, like India, might find its role in the world greatly diminished.

These perceptions have contributed to and been reinforced by disappointments in the economic area. Many joint ventures have been discussed, but few have weathered the process of development such that real returns may be reported, to say nothing of profitable results.

From the beginning, the presumption has been that there was enough "social energy" in the rank and file of Russian society to impel the transformation forward, and that it only needed tapping. Along with the early period of euphoria about potential Soviet-Western economic growth came a rush of Western "think tanks" and other agglomerations of experts, offering advice on the rapid transformation of the Russian internal market. Yet none of the proposals tendered to Soviet leadership has proven workable, and not one of the basic problems of the system has been resolved.

Privatisation of state owned enterprises is still a dream. The central issue of land tenure has not been addressed.

In his 1987 text, Rumsfeld emphasized, "we would be mistaken to perceive change in the Soviet Union as a process resembling change in the U.S." This seems to be the key to the matter; change is more or less continuous in the West, but in the East change has been slow and spasmodic. With the rise of Communist ideology, and its rejection of conscience and morality in favour of absolute obedience to the elite, a tendency to change direction in a whimsical or panicky fashion became more pronounced.

In addition to wild swings in policy, Soviet rule has been characterized by contradictions that cannot but appear to be products, if not of deliberate deceit, then of a remarkable failure to understand the meaning and consequences of one's actions.

With the leadership seemingly incapable of developing responsible policies that would lead to the exercise of meaningful direction, nothing in the post-Soviet conundrum is more troubling to Americans than the threat of a colossal break-up on ethnic lines, with the emergence of new warring states and armies.

–Arguments and Facts International, June-July 1991

Russia's *Tejerazo*

In the counterrevolutionary coup attempt launched in Moscow in August 1991, Communist Party reactionaries inadvertently accomplished a goal central to the success of the reformist programme they sought to oppose. Staking everything on a recovery of the party dictatorship, they wrecked the party as a leading political force.

Thus, they removed a major obstacle to the full democratisation of post-Soviet political life and the privatisation of the economy.

An immediate consequence has been a revival of U.S. business interest in the post-Soviet economy. In the wake of Boris Yeltsin's victory, the Associated Press reported, "The failure of the Soviet coup may renew confidence among corporations considering investments there and prompt Western nations to increase economic aid to the troubled nation...

"Several companies that have sunk money into the Soviet Union said they were not fazed by the events of the past few days and believe that they may lead to greater economic reform. 'I have a lot of confidence that good will happen from this,' said Aileen Exeter, a vice president of MBL International, a ComputerLand franchisee that has built five ComputerLand stores in the Soviet Union. She said her company is proceeding with plans for two more stores there by the end of the year. USWest, the regional phone company that is building a cellular phone system in Moscow, also does not believe the coup attempt will disrupt its business... Economist Sean O'Neill of WEFA Group, another economic forecasting firm, agreed that the coup attempt could speed economic reform."

At the same time, Reuters noted that "the news sparked optimism in grain markets that trade between the United States and the Soviet Union will quickly return to normal... The Soviet Union is the most important market for U.S. farm exports, accounting for six per cent of agricultural trade and 18 per cent of the corn exported."

The failed coup, although it took the world by surprise, had its curious precedents. One was the June-July assault on Slovenia and Croatia by the Yugoslav armed forces; numerous Western European press organs warned that the supine attitude of the democracies to this attack would encourage hardliners in Moscow. (1)

More remarkable was the similarity between the *Yanayevshchina*, the attempted Communist restoration, and the *Tejerazo*, the effort by fascist minded military and police to overthrow the democratised regime in Spain in 1981. In both cases, the remnants of a dead dictatorship attempted to regain power by brute force, but failed to understand that centrist political leaders would join with the majority in opposing them.

The coup plotters in both Spain and Russia misjudged the stance of apparent "figureheads" such as King Juan Carlos and Mikhail

---

(1) On the Yugoslav collapse and ensuing wars, the reader is directed to the author's *Kosovo: Background to a War*, also published by Anthem Press.

Gorbachev, who proved committed to a modern, democratic identity for each of their nations. A new stable European or American style state represented the only hope for either country's full entry into the world economy.

The "Spanish transition" after Franco's death has many other lessons to offer the countries in the East now undergoing a "grand transition." The operative principle in the successful transition away from dictatorial rule, in Spain's case, has been that of the clean slate, with former state and party bureaucrats shielded from reprisals for past brutalities, but obliged to adopt new careers in the private sector and in civil society. Trials and purges were imposed only on those who broke the law.

This conciliatory approach to individuals and political tendencies – emulated in such other "transition" states as post-Pinochet Chile and Nicaragua after the electoral defeat of the Sandinistas – will have to be adopted in the new Russia. There is no alternative, unless the country is to undergo years of recurring, uncontrollable conflict.

However, Juan Tomás de Salas, editor of Spain's leading news-magazine, *Cambio16*, has pointed out a major difference between Spain and Russia.

Spain's post-Franco democracy succeeded in striking roots in society largely because the task of dismantling the Falangist command economy had been accomplished years before Franco's death, by the group of technocrats associated with the Catholic conservative movement *Opus Dei*. No such group has existed in Russia, and the task of economic reform there remains an extremely daunting one.

The main political institution erected during the Bolshevik era, the party-state, may now be completely removed from the environment. But some cultural obstacles to an economic transformation will persist, and although America's business community is once again excited about Russian reform, serious investment projects will face immense difficulties.

Unlike Bolshevik totalitarianism, the Franco variety did not punish enterprise or liquidate the middle class or discourage productivity. All these phenomena of Soviet culture have combined to trouble the reconstitution of the Russian economy.

There is a seldom-mentioned irony here, in that Lenin's New Economic Policy, beginning in 1921, saw a much easier and more efficient "restoration of capitalism" than Yeltsin is likely to achieve. The moral being that even after revolution and civil war early Bolshevism had not yet wiped out the spirit of individual initiative, and once the peasants and traders were allowed to resume private market operations, they did so successfully.

The 60 years of Communist repression – ranging from mass deportations of the so-called "kulaks" to execution of "speculators" to discrimination against Jews and Caucasian peoples, all expressions of crude anticapitalism – have taken their toll. With the political supports for such policies removed, incentives to eradicate the habits they created must still emerge.

–Arguments and Facts International, August-September 1991

Second Thoughts

San Francisco

While the much ballyhooed Mikhail Gorbachev Foundation (now called the State of the World Forum) has carried out an ongoing media campaign to establish itself as a global think tank, a clash of cultures has emerged between Gorbachev and his U.S. associates on one side, and on the other, a number of long serving anti-Communist scholars and policy experts at the powerful Hoover Institution, based at Stanford University in California.

During his spring 1992 U.S. tour, Gorbachev reportedly raised millions of dollars for his foundation. But the activities of the organization and of its U.S. branch, the Gorbachev Foundation USA, have come under scrutiny by members of the policy community that originally seemed to support its creation.

"The Gorbachev Foundation is the propagation of a falsehood," declared Angelo Codevilla, a Hoover veteran, formerly with the U.S. Senate Intelligence Committee. "They are giving the American public the impression that the Cold War ended and the Communist regime fell because of Gorbachev and his American friends, when he and they actually did everything possible to keep the system going."

Codevilla described the Gorbachev Foundation as "portraying the end of the Cold War as the product of meetings between U.S. and Russian elite figures, likeminded types who just decided it wasn't worth it anymore, when Communism fell because of Russians in the street, not the elite."

"Gorbachev is a superstar, and some people may be using him for their own motives," said John Dunlop, a nine year Hoover senior fellow and expert on Russian ethnic issues. "I think Gorbachev's Western friends are sincere, and that there is an objective basis for the adulation directed to him. He is perceived as the man who greatly reduced the danger of a nuclear exchange, and therefore as a man of peace."

But Dunlop continued, "The irony is that Gorbachev continues to enjoy this enormous esteem in the West while in his own country he is extremely unpopular. I think it's clear that the purpose of the Gorbachev Foundation is not only to promote Gorbachev but also to promote the platform he stands for, which is one of renewed socialism and reestablishment of the former Soviet Union. I believe he remains a Marxist-Leninist, and that he has yet to acquiesce to the formation of the Commonwealth of Independent States. These are the views promoted by the Foundation.

"Why isn't there a Yeltsin Foundation?" Dunlop asked. "This is the man who stands closest to the fundamental beliefs that we Americans adhere to: pluralism, multiparty democracy, and a market economy in a westward-looking Russia. Gorbachev is a man of the past. He's a reform Communist in the post-Communist age. What's the point of a Gorbachev Foundation?

"Gorbachev should be playing the role of an elder statesman, rather than indulging himself in the delusion that, like Charles de Gaulle, he will be recalled to power. He is definitely playing a very dangerous game in his attacks on Yeltsin," Dunlop said.

The U.S. branch of the Foundation, based in San Francisco, has received considerable media attention and anticipated large donations thanks to support from such individuals as George Shultz, former secretary of state.

In addition to Shultz, the group claimed the endorsement of no less than Ronald Reagan, although some associates of the Foundation continue to attack Reagan and his policies.

"I just don't think Shultz really understands what's going on," commented another Hoover personality, who requested anonymity.

Prominent figures at Hoover have also criticized the involvement in the Gorbachev Foundation of personalities from California's "New

Age" subculture, symbolized by Foundation director James Garrison. Garrison was a founder of the Christic Institute, which was fined $1.7 million (£1.05 million) for filing a "frivolous" lawsuit against the U.S. government, and was a long-time functionary of the "hot tub" Esalen Institute.

The Gorbachev Foundation's "New Age" posture led to an involvement with individuals like professor John Mack, a tenured faculty member in psychiatry at the Harvard Medical School in Massachusetts.

Mack, who acted as moderator at a San Francisco seminar on "Esalen Diplomacy With the Soviets, 1979-1992," had publicly affirmed his belief that a "huge, strange interspecies or interbeing breeding program has invaded our physical reality and is affecting the lives of hundreds of thousands, if not millions of people, and in some way the consciousness of the entire planet."

Mack claimed this subversive plan was behind stories of U.F.O. "abductions" of innocent earthlings, and told one observer at the seminar that people in "the U.F.O. community" believe Gorbachev himself had a "contact experience" with a U.F.O.

Mack was publicly accused by nuclear physicist Edward Teller of promoting a K.G.B. campaign to undermine U.S. science and defence research.

In the view of Garrison, Esalen directors Michael and Dulce Murphy, and their cohort, the "New Age" approach was not only a motive force for Soviet change, its strategy was successful because it was specifically opposed to the tough policies pursued by Reagan. That is, the hot tubbers "kept the faith" and defied the Reagan line of limited contact with the Soviet regime, and glasnost succeeded because the hot tub "diplomats" were unafraid to "embrace" the K.G.B.

"I am not at all surprised that Garrison would have a background with something like the Christic Institute," said Codevilla. "But it is all the more surprising to see establishment thinkers associating themselves with such an enterprise" as the Gorbachev Foundation.

At the time of Gorbachev's 1992 visit to San Francisco, there were already some bad omens for the project. They included a repudiation of the effort by Henry Kissinger, whose name was listed as a sponsor of the tour, but who reportedly said he knew nothing about it, except that he offered to hold a small breakfast event.

Then came the resignation from the sponsors' list of Ambassador Arthur Hartman, the top U.S. diplomat in Moscow during much of the early glasnost period. Hartman, who is well acquainted with the movers and shakers of the Foundation, as well as with Gorbachev himself, refused to support a money raising effort without guarantees as to how the funds would be spent.

–Arguments and Facts International, September-October 1992

Eva Hoffman's *Exit Into History:* A Review

Eva Hoffman, a former editor of *The New York Times Book Review,* has produced a curiously old-fashioned book, based on her visits in 1990 and 1991 to the "inner ring" of East European states – Poland, Czecho-Slovakia (still a unit), Hungary, Romania, and Bulgaria. Her account lacks depth, and has the quality of a greatly extended article for the American magazine *National Geographic,* offering semi-photographic impressions of vaguely defined cultural environments, through the comments of "representative," i.e. stereotypical, local personalities.

This genre of journalism has become somewhat passé in recent years as the collapse of Communism has not only opened up enormous resources for the study of hitherto-suppressed political, economic, and social history in the former East Bloc "buffer zone," but has also made the mastery of such recent data seem urgent, given the deep crises and threats of war emanating therefrom.

Ms. Hoffman visited the then-five, now six countries in the period when Communism had ceased to function as an ideological system, but when the post-Communist order had yet to be clearly defined. She describes a Poland in which the revolutionary alliance of the Solidarity labour union and independent intellectuals had fought the regime to a standstill. She then goes to Czecho-Slovakia, and makes Prague and the Czech lands sound a great deal more drab than one might assume from the starry-eyed enthusiasm of the quasi-intellectual "new expatriates" who have flocked there. She finds something comfortingly reminiscent of her native Poland in Slovakia, edging toward national independence, although she is perturbed to hear revisionist claims in favour of Mons. Josef Tiso, the Slovak nationalist who headed a pro-Nazi puppet regime in World War II.

In Hungary, she briefly encounters, at the Budapest train station, the semi-Asian peasant reality of the wide Pannonian plain. The station is filled with gypsies and peasants in wild costume, with fruit and vegetables on sale everywhere. But she presents without resonance her shift from the more sedate Slavic world of the Poles, Czechs, and Slovaks to the exotic Magyar culture, with its linguistic roots close to the Turks and Mongols of Central Asia and a grand (and recent) imperial past. She comments on the change in sensibility, but offers almost nothing in the way of background to fill out the picture.

She then proceeds to a hellish Romania where her understanding of events is clearly handicapped by her not knowing the local language. There she takes note of a fascist style of ultranationalism that, as in Slovakia, harks back to the frenzies of the Hitler era while, for any current reader, also providing chilling notes in anticipation of the slaughter in former Yugoslavia.

Bulgaria as she describes it appears to have suffered remarkably little under Communism, and also lacks the nationalist irritability of its neighbours, notwithstanding conflicts involving its indigenous Muslim population, who suffered the indignity of being forced to adopt Christian names under Communism.

Ms. Hoffman is Jewish, and Jewish concerns are a subtext in this book, although perhaps too subordinated, for it would have been better to more thoroughly research and document the situation of Jews in all these countries. One of the few really interesting anecdotes, of the many presented in this volume, recounts the alleged practice of Polish peasants who, not knowing the history of Jews buried in a local cemetery, pray at the long abandoned gravestones in the belief that they shelter "wise men, magicians perhaps." However, this has more than a bit of the flavour of an urban legend.

There is little in this book that is very surprising. Most of it revisits the predictable, symbolic ground of the Communist era: shabby apartments, hostile service workers, brave but self-questioning anti-regime intellectuals, occasional inchoate outbursts of resurgent anti-Semitism and nationalist extremism. This landscape is so familiar it threatens to become a cliché, at the same time as we must imagine it disappearing, at least in some places.

Unfortunately, along with this lack of novelty go sloppy editing, occasional errors, and some statements that are downright wrong. For example, any competent editor should have been able to clarify who the Knights of Malta, the Catholic charity organization active in Poland, are. Ms. Hoffman had never heard of them before.

Ms. Hoffman is the author of a previous book, *Lost in Translation*, about her experience as a bilingual writer in Polish and English. Sadly, much of the dialogue in this work seems also to have become lost in translation, with some of it rendered genuinely incomprehensible.

–*World Affairs Council Booknotes (San Francisco), May 1994*

Mexican Venona:
The "Gnome" Affair

The word *Venona* has no meaning. It is a cipher invented by American professional codebreakers to cover one of the most remarkable episodes in 20th century history: the decryption of some 2,900 secret communications, recorded from 1940 to 1948, between Moscow and the Soviet intelligence posts throughout the world – commercial, diplomatic, N.K.V.D./K.G.B and military/naval (G.R.U.) From the beginning of the work undertaken by military code-breakers in the U.S., at the outset of World War II, the project was successively hidden with names chosen by American and British officials in the hope of keeping it under a maximum degree of confidentiality. These included ACORN, BRIDE, DINAR, DRUG, EIDER, JADE, and TRINE.

Among American academics and journalists the existence of Venona has been known for the past 30 years; in the middle of the 1960s historians specializing in the American response to N.K.V.D./K.G.B. activities revealed the existence of a corpus of messages that supported the accusations against the Rosenberg couple, Alger Hiss, and other Soviet agents. Nevertheless, it was understood that the U.S. authorities had never introduced the information gained from Venona into court proceedings in those cases, and that many years would have to pass before major details of them would come before the public.

In any event, the fall of the Soviet Union, the partial and ambiguous opening of Moscow archives, and other considerations led the U.S. National Security Agency, the institution charged with intelligence affairs related to communications and codes, to begin publication of the Venona archive in 1994. The first of six releases, plus analytical documents, included messages related to atomic espionage during World War II, obviously the most controversial issue in Cold War history. Four more releases, up to 1996, included materials mainly originating in N.K.V.D. residencies in London, Stockholm, New York, Washington, San Francisco, and Mexico City, along with G.R.U. and naval G.R.U. stations in London, New York, and Washington.

The specialist historiography of Soviet espionage since 1989 has tended to distinguish between the work of the European academics, who have concentrated on Stalinism in the 1930s and its effect on the Communist International or Comintern, and that of the U.S. experts who have been almost exclusively interested in the Cold War. For Mexico and Spain the most important, by far, of the Venona releases was the fourth, in summer 1996, which consisted in 850 messages, comprising communications between the N.K.V.D. in Moscow, Mexico City, and San Francisco. The grouping of the latter cities may or may not have been coincidental; as I sought to demonstrate in my book *From West to East: California and the Making of the American Mind*, a longstanding geographical logic, and even tradition, had made San Francisco a centre of overseas Soviet intelligence equal to New York, beginning in the late 1920s. For at least a decade thereafter, and even at the time of the Trotsky assassination in 1940, Mexico City lacked a Soviet embassy or other diplomatic mission to support a major N.K.V.D. network. In addition, the Mexican Communist Party, the natural adjunct to the Soviet diplomatic structure in the pursuit of espionage and terror, had been kept subordinate to the American Communist Party by Moscow. Thus, most of the conspiracy to kill Trotsky was organized on U.S. soil, with San Francisco a key location.

The N.K.V.D. communications from Mexico revealed the notably obsessive nature of Soviet secret operations and the extent of their penetration and manipulations throughout Latin America, which involved the Spanish Republican exile community as well as many prominent intellectuals, along with the Communist Parties of Mexico, Chile, Cuba, and other countries.

The Venona archive also showed the degree of criminal activities undertaken by international Soviet agents, who operated throughout the world, on the U.S. West Coast as well as in Mexico or Colombia, as if they were on their own territory. These agents pursued, kidnapped, and murdered Russian citizens who had escaped the Stalinist terror, stole the secrets of industrial and scientific enterprises, and corrupted foreign political and military personnel.

But before reviewing the highlights of the Mexican Venona, it is worthwhile discussing the deeper semiotics of Venona. The Venona archive is an agglomeration of texts that lends itself in a unique manner to post-modern analysis, although few contemporary literary critics or academic theorists would seem to be interested in such a task. The shape and form of the communications throws considerable light on the mental processes and habitual structures that characterized N.K.V.D. activities. Indeed, much of the vocabulary of the codes found in Venona features curious and even entertaining subtextual elements.

For example, in the greater part of the Venona archive the U.S. is designated "the country" (*stran'*) while its cities take the names of the great capitals of the Phoenician, Carthaginian and other extinct civilizations. Washington is "Carthage," New York is "Tyre," and San Francisco, marvellously, is "Babylon." Perhaps by association, London appears as "Sidon," while Great Britain is, predictably, "the island" (*ostrog*). Canada is "Forestland" (*Lesovia*) while Mexico figures as *dyeryevnya*, "the countryside" or "rural area." A new term, "the village" (*selo*) appears repeatedly beginning in 1944 and seems to refer to Guatemala.

To illustrate their contempt for the U.S. authorities, the label chosen by the N.K.V.D. for the U.S. Office of Strategic Services, the forerunner of the Central Intelligence Agency, is "the log cabin" (*izba*) while the F.B.I. is "the hut" (*khata*). The apparent intention was to emphasize the primitive nature of these U.S. security agencies when compared to the mighty Soviet organizations; but one also must smile, at least, to imagine the reaction of American codebreakers dealing with these insults. By contrast, other foreign intelligence or police agencies (including those of Mexico and Guatemala) were typically known as "the competitors;" the British security services were respectfully denominated "the island competitors," implying no malicious humour. Soviet military intelligence, the G.R.U. or Main Intelligence Directorate of the Red or Soviet Army, appeared under the traditional term, "the neighbours."

The local Communist Party in most countries was known as "the corporation," while its members were always designated with an extremely revealing title: "the compatriots" or "the fellowcountrymen" (*zemlyaki*). This is the most interesting of all the Venona lexical items from the viewpoint of linguistic analysis. To begin with, it illustrates that foreign Communists were considered tantamount to Soviet citizens. It also seems to have something in common with the Yiddish expression *landsman,* or "fellow Jew." But *landsman* bears within itself a dual origin and significance. Its Hebrew equivalent, *am haaretz* or "man of the land," also means "man of the soil," or "peasant," with a further shading as "simpleton" or "bumpkin." These levels do not exist in the Russian *zemlyak,* but they may, in the end, denote the real image Soviet Communists had of their foreign counterparts.

The exiled Spanish Republican government headed by Juan Negrín, the Fidel Castro of his time, was known as "the building" or "the construction." In dealing with its nongovernmental enemies, the N.K.V.D. engaged in a sinister comedy, referring to the Trotskyists as "polecats" and the Zionists as "rats."

The *klichki* or individual aliases assigned to agents at times reflected an equally macabre sense of humour, even when the majority of common "workers," or first-level agents, had *klichki* without particularly obvious associations. For example, the frightful Lavrenti Pavlovich Beria, supreme chief of the N.K.V.D., was known only as "Petrov." The Soviet ambassador in Mexico, Konstantin Umanskii, was "the editor," probably alluding to his previous activities as a foreign correspondent for the Soviet press.

At the same time, Pavel Mikhailov, an outstanding G.R.U. spy working in New York, was given the prestigious alias "Molière." Grigory Kheifitz, N.K.V.D. *rezident* or local chief in San Francisco, was known as "Charon," a homage to the mythical boatman of the dead, an extremely appropriate *klichka* given that a large part of his work consisted of the capture and return to Russia, to a certain death, of sailors who had deserted from Soviet ships tied up in U.S. West Coast ports.

Although the N.K.V.D. did not establish a *rezidentura* in Mexico City until 1943, many communications from New York to Moscow dealt, before that date, with affairs in Mexico. In Mexico City the single most important N.K.V.D. operative was none other than Jaume Raimon Mercader del Rio, the assassin of Trotsky, who happened to be in prison. Mercader was known as "Gnome" and "Rita," an example of the intelligence world's penchant for androgyny in the interest of encipherment.

From the beginning of its operations the Mexico City *rezidentura* gave top priority to breaking Mercader out of jail. The project was referred to under multiple names, utilizing a supplementary system of coding, and involved parallel plans for a violent flight, or an escape effected through corruption of Mexican officials. The existence of such intentions on the part of the N.K.V.D. in Mexico has been remarked on by historians of the Trotsky assassination since the 1950s, suggesting the rare disclosure of a small part of the Venona corpus at an early date, at least to Mexican police officials.

The first message regarding the efforts to free Mercader, transmitted from Mexico City to Moscow on December 23, 1943, refer to the rescue of Mercader as "the surgical operation." This terminology obviously derives from the common use of the term "hospital," for a prison, in the old jargon of revolutionary conspirators and spies. A prison sentence would become an "illness" or a "stay in the hospital." However, later messages, dated December 29 and 30, 1943 and January 3, 1944, disclose an entirely new vocabulary of cover words.

The overall plan for the liberation of Mercader was renamed the "repair job," and later, the "achievement." The "hospital" became the "laboratory," the escape plan became the "mixture," the courtroom the "storeroom," and the escape route the "theory." A reduction in the number of participants became a "drop in the temperature," a house was an "author," a car, "soda" (a chemical) and the Mexican N.K.V.D. agents were "scientists."

In yet another demonstration of the weird sense of humour, or, perhaps, the use of contradictory terminology comparable to the assignment of female names to males, smuggling was referred to as "direct transmission" and the action itself described as the "test." Further messages show the return to the use of the term "hospital" for the Lecumberri Penitentiary where Mercader was held.

The list of Mexican "scientists" controlled by the N.K.V.D. is long and includes many names of no significance to the rest of the world. But one also finds therein an individual coded as *kon'* – "chess knight," according to American decryption, although the Russian word could also be translated more simply and convincingly as "the horse," which figures, in the Hispanic world, as *caballo,* a macho nickname for one who flaunts his masculinity. In any case, the American identification of this *klichka* with the noted painter David Alfaro Siqueiros seems unarguable. Siqueiros had been the leader of the first, unsuccessful attempt on Trotsky's life, in May 1940, and then escaped to Chile with help from the Chilean diplomat and poet Pablo Neruda, who was posted to Mexico City.

Telegraphic and surface communications between Moscow and Mexico City were supplemented by clandestine radio communications from Khabarovsk, in Siberia, as well as from the Soviet capital.

An especially active N.K.V.D. agent in Mexico was the exiled Spanish author and feminist Margarita Nelken, known under the *klichka* "Amor," or, in Spanish, "love." Nelken was something of a world figure in her time. Her tasks for Soviet intelligence in Mexico were considerable and included a mission as liaison, described in a message dated March 31, 1944, with an unknown person, "Mateo," to explore the establishment of an independent apparatus, controlled exclusively by the N.K.V.D., to carry out illegal border crossing operations from Mexico into the U.S. Such illegal entries were common, and operated in both directions; Soviet spies were also landed on the U.S. West Coast and then crossed into Mexico, with the complicity of a local Mexican military commander.

Nelken was but one of a great number of Spanish Republicans who worked as Soviet agents in Mexico, the U.S., France, and elsewhere. She was linked to the conspiracy to free Mercader, as well as to Caridad Mercader, or "Klava," the assassin's mother. "Klava" herself was the recipient of numerous messages from Moscow, some of them regarding her other sons, Luis, who then lived in Russia, and Jorge, who at the end of World War II was found to have survived a Nazi concentration camp. Behind the scenes of the plot to get Mercader out of prison we find N.K.V.D. general Naum Eitingon, or "Tom," the former lover of "Klava" and the director of the Trotsky murder. We also find the N.K.V.D. bigwigs extremely concerned that inter-

44

nal squabbles among the Spanish Communist leaders in Mexico would endanger the Mercader breakout.

Along with the Spanish Republicans a considerable number of Chileans appear in Venona, beginning in May 1942 with Neruda, and including his successor as Chilean consul in Mexico City, Luis Enrique Delano.

The plot to liberate Mercader represented an obvious violation of Mexican national sovereignty. Such incidents occurred in an environment of continuous abuse of Mexican passports, government agencies, and resources, for conspiratorial ends. Soviet spies were dispatched to the "countryside" to fabricate "legends" or false identities in anticipation of their secure entry into the U.S. and Britain. With such goals in mind, according to a message from Moscow to Mexico City dated September 10, 1944, Mexican or Guatemalan identity documents were considered preferable to Canadian papers, probably because the falsity of the latter was easier to check.

The N.K.V.D. maintained an active interest in many and varied political targets on Mexican soil. The long list of enemies is eloquently presented in a message from Moscow to Mexico City dated June 11, 1945, a few days before a massive victory parade scheduled in Moscow to celebrate the end of the war. This communiqué, sent simultaneously to N.K.V.D. stations in Algiers, Bogotá, Brussels, London, Montevideo, New York, Ottawa, Paris, San Francisco, Tokyo, Washington, and Zagreb, prohibits the issuance of visas to any nondiplomatic foreigner for a period of 11 days from June 15 to June 25.

The communiqué additionally demands special vigilance to avoid that any of the following elements might utilize the occasion of the victory celebration to infiltrate the Soviet Union "on terrorist missions:" white Russian émigrés, nationalists (i.e. Ukrainians or Armenians), Trotskyists, Zionists, priests, veterans of the "national legions" (presumably volunteers who had joined the German armies), Mensheviks, Russian Constitutional Democrats, and monarchists. A later message demands a survey and analysis of the presence in Mexico City (no doubt extremely marginal) of Russians, Ukrainians, Belarusians, Armenians, Georgians, mountain folk from the northern Caucasus, Central Asians, and Balts who might have emigrated from the U.S.S.R. One can only add that to conceive of a northern Caucasian mountaineer, say a Chechen or Daghestani, living in Mexico City, is to stray into an area to which only literature, and that of a high imaginative order, could possibly do justice.

That the majority of these "anti-Soviet elements," such as Trotskyists, Mensheviks, Constitutional Democrats, and monarchists, were politically and organizationally on the edge of extinction in 1945, and that they had little or no presence in Mexico, to say nothing of Bogotá or Montevideo, seems to have been irrelevant to the N.K.V.D. bosses in Moscow. In any case, thousands of refugees from the Soviet Union had attempted to remain in Western Europe, and some must have escaped to the Western Hemisphere. Polish exiles in Mexico were followed and surveilled to gauge the utility of clandestine operations against them. Nevertheless, the apprehensions of Moscow regarding such minuscule groups must appear as absurdly exaggerated. As an additional example, Moscow commanded on February 21, 1945 that the N.K.V.D. in Mexico City report on "the reaction of Armenian circles," presumably in the capital, to a synod of the Armenian Orthodox Church that had been held in the monastery of Echmiadzin in Armenia.

The irrational character of N.K.V.D. orders is especially obvious in the continued persecution of Natalya Ivanovna Sedova, the isolated and psychologically bereft widow of the murdered Trotsky. And in this instance we encounter anew some of the outstanding personalities from among the "killerati" employed in the "Western assault" in Europe almost ten years before, as described in the first chapter of the present volume.

After the 1940 slaying, Sedova lived for 20 years more in the little "house" on the calle Viena, which, except for its walled garden, appears as more a stone cabin than a house, a narrow and somewhat claustrophobic space inhabited by the couple for a year and a half before the killing. Her circle was small. Apart from Trotskyist militants such as the Mexican writer Manuel Fernández Grandizo (G. Munis), and other exiles like Victor Serge, Sedova received few visitors and none of influence in the outside world. Even so, the N.K.V.D. maintained a rigorous scrutiny over her activities.

The network established by the N.K.V.D. with the intent of freeing Mercader had extended to other localities, with some messages sent from Bogotá and San Francisco, reflecting a concern that the "achievement" be postponed beyond its original deadline. At the same time, the surveillance of Natalya Sedova was detailed in messages sent by the N.K.V.D. from New York, from where the penetration of the Trotskyist movement was coordinated, utilizing a number of exceptionally fearsome agents.

One of these was Mordechai "Mark" Zborowski ("Tulip" or "Kant" in Venona), the Ukrainian Jew responsible, in Europe in the late '30s, for the theft of a part of Trotsky's archives and the methodical poisoning of Trotsky's son, Lev Sedov. In addition, Zborowski was an accomplice in the N.K.V.D. assassinations, during the "Western assault," of the N.K.V.D. defector Ignacy Porecki (Ignace Reiss), the Catalan author Andreu Nin, leader of the dissident Marxist P.O.U.M., the Trotskyist militants Erwin Wolf and Rudolf Klement, and the white Russian exile Gen. Yevgeny Karlovich Miller.

In 1940 Zborowski had fled from Europe to New York, where he gained employment as an anthropological researcher while secretly surveilling and harassing Soviet dissidents, including a famous defector of that time, Victor Kravchenko (denoted "Gnat" by the N.K.V.D., with typical low humour, in Venona.) But the team of N.K.V.D. terror specialists then working in New York may also have included one of Zborowski's most vicious colleagues. According to *The Mitrokhin Archive*, published in 1999, the N.K.V.D. *rezident* in New York in mid-1945, Vladimir Sergeevich Pravdin, with the *klichka* "Sergei," was actually Roland Abbiate, a French citizen who directed the tracking and murder of Ignace Reiss. Pravdin is a prominent character in Venona, but the ascription of a French identity to him is not included in the American documentation. If Pravdin was indeed Abbiate, then the skeleton of the "mobile unit" that wreaked havoc in Europe years before had been effectively transferred to the U.S. Certainly, Zborowski and Abbiate would have had much about which they could reminisce, little of it very pleasant. But the reconstitution of the terror squad on American territory, with Naum Eitingon, or "Tom," always in the wings, has other, more chilling implications.

It is certainly clear from Venona that the hunting down and liquidation of Trotskyists was a goal of the N.K.V.D. that far exceeded many others in importance. The whole matter evinces a logic so bizarre and a temperament so perverse that most people unacquainted with Stalinist psychology would doubtless be tempted to disbelieve it, sixty years later. After the Trotsky murder, the eponymous movement was a tiny force with almost no political impact anywhere in the world. It had considerable numbers, briefly, in Greece and Vietnam, before its cadres were physically wiped out by Communist guerrillas in both countries at the end of World War II. Indeed, in Vietnam it was a revolutionary movement that offered serious competition to the Viet Minh. But Vietnam was far from Moscow and even further from Paris and New York, then still considered the probable centres of a new "world revolution." Few people in New York, even intellectuals, knew where Vietnam was in 1945, and the slaughter of the Trotskyist militants there caused a ripple in Trotskyist newspapers, but no other echo. The massacre of the Greek Trotskyists, a bit closer to the revolutionary mecca of Paris, at least, also drew almost no attention, since few leftists of that time outside Greece could read Greek or had any interest in the internal politics of the revolutionary movement there.

Trotskyists also had a mass following in Bolivia and Sri Lanka, neither of them central factors in regional politics. Trotskyists tended to flourish in countries that the Soviets considered of secondary or tertiary importance. We know beyond doubt that Stalin had written off the serious option of a Communist revolution in Greece, although that did not stop his mercenaries from killing their radical rivals. But in the Muscovite scheme of things, China was obviously more important than Vietnam, India more significant than Sri Lanka, and Brazil and Argentina more substantial targets than Bolivia.

Trotskyism was, however, a dangerous undertaking in France at that time. With the end of the war, French Communist Partisans had liquidated tens of thousands of "enemies" as ostensible Nazi collaborators, including an Italian Trotskyist, Pietro Tresso, known as "Blasco." In addition, although Trotskyism was hardly a major movement in the U.S., it had commanded the loyalty of a major section of the Teamsters' Union, the powerful organization of truck drivers in the American Midwest, as well as the dominant union of seamen on the U.S. West Coast, and it was a fashionable trend among radical intellectuals in New York. For Trotskyists around the world, then, America, ironically enough, was the lighthouse of the revolution.

The operations of Zborowski and, allegedly, Abbiate in New York in 1945 must be seen in that context. For Stalin and the N.K.V.D. America was perhaps less immediately important in the struggle for global leadership than as a nest of the hated "polecats." This would have changed dramatically, of course, once the Soviets grasped that American president Harry Truman was not inclined to accommodate Stalin. But with veterans of the "Western assault" active in Manhattan, the lives of many independent leftist intellectuals were very likely in much greater danger than many people would have thought. And the success of the American military codebreakers, along with the vigilance of the F.B.I., may have had a completely unanticipated, unknown, and, to many, an inconceivable outcome: the protection of American radicals from the N.K.V.D.

Venona shows conclusively that the N.K.V.D. had thoroughly infiltrated Trotskyist ranks in America and regularly intercepted Trotskyist communications. One agent, Floyd C. Miller, had the Venona *klichka* "Khe…," an apparently meaningless symbol that could be interpreted as the English "he." Miller acted as a Trotskyist liaison with the anti-Stalinist labour leaders in the maritime industry, as well as visiting Trotsky's widow in Mexico City. Miller had proposed to the New York Trotskyists that Sedova could be taken across the U.S. border into Texas, where one cannot exclude the possibility of an attempted liquidation. But Miller was apparently not the only agent actively spying on Sedova. In the meantime, another veteran of the "Western assault," the Catalan Communist named Victori Salà, a key figure in the suppression of the P.O.U.M. in the Spanish civil war, had surfaced in Mexico City and, of course, appeared in the Venona traffic.

For Moscow, the entire series of operations was important not only in itself, but also for the progress of the conspiracy to free Mercader. The "Gnome" project, as it came to be called, was developed in incredible detail, including the purchase of a motor launch. But the plan also encountered obstacles, above all in the form of the assassin's mother, "Klava," who had become a real nuisance. In a message dated March 9 and 10, 1945, Moscow insisted, on the basis of concern for her physical safety, that "the presence of Klava in the countryside gravely compromises the Gnome project;" i.e., the assassin's mother was meddling in the preparations. It has long been known that Caridad Mercader had made her son's escape the centre of all her concerns.

In effect, the entire operation seemed to have fallen into complete disorder. A message from the KGB *rezident* in San Francisco, Grigori Kasparov ("Gift"), to Beria in Moscow, dated August 19, 1944, offers an extensive criticism of the Mexico City *rezident*, a certain Tarasov ("Yuri"), for his handling of the "Gnome" plan. "My work with him has demonstrated to me that the case is in inexpert and indecisive hands," Kasparov complained. Tarasov had "abandoned work and driven 90 kilometres to his country house for three or four days, preventing the coordination of urgent tasks." Kasparov had tried to speed up the liberation of Mercader, but Tarasov wasted too much time in useless exercises, while living a luxurious life with servants, in a house with a big garden, where he had taken to raising exotic birds. (One wonders if Kasparov's life in "Babylon," the city by the Golden Gate, was any more ascetic.) Since San Francisco was considered more important than Mexico City in the N.K.V.D. structural hierarchy, it had fallen to Kasparov to try to correct matters.

Soviet discussion of these misadventures continued for some time, but Mercader was not freed until 1960, when he had completed his sentence in the Trotsky murder – 20 years, the maximum under Mexican law. He journeyed first to Cuba, then to Russia, then back to Cuba, where he died in 1978, though he was apparently buried in Russia.

Venona is a whole continent, and its Mexican aspect is but a section of its fascinating landscape. It reveals much about the attitudes and habits, as much as the methods, of Stalin's secret police. This terrifying body functioned as a parallel government not only in Russia, but in other countries where it operated, including Mexico. It created identities, took lives, hired and fired spies, and above all mercilessly tracked its enemies, regardless of their power or lack thereof.

Thanks to Venona and the military codebreakers of the U.S., the work of the K.G.B. and its predecessors, of a kind that we will likely never see again, is now known, as never before.

–Vuelta (Mexico City), August 1997
Translated from Spanish by the author

Chapter III:

STALINIST RUSSIA AND THE JEWS

Inside a Purge:
"All Jews Were Useless Riffraff"

Publication in Russia of the transcripts from the secret trial of the Jewish Anti-Fascist Committee (J.A.F.C.), whose members were among the last to die in Stalin's purges, has opened up a lost chapter in the history of Communism and its war on Jews.

Unlike other recent releases of Soviet documents, which have been haphazard and often more confusing than clarifying, the 400-page volume on the J.A.F.C. sheds new light on the annihilation of this group of leftwing Jewish intellectuals. The document was issued with the imprimatur of Boris Yeltsin himself, by the official Presidential Commission of the Russian Federation for the Rehabilitation of Victims of Political Repression.

"It is one of the key documents on anti-Semitism in our time," said Robert Conquest, doyen of historians of Stalinism and a fellow at the Hoover Institution. Conquest has called for the rapid translation of the book into English. Entitled *Unjust Trial: The Last Stalinist Executions,* the stenographic record from the 1952 trial was edited by historian V.P. Naumov and issued by the Russian publisher Nauka. It is being distributed in the West, but so far only in Russian.

The Jewish Anti-Fascist Committee was set up by the Soviets in 1942 at the suggestion of Viktor Alter and Henryk Erlykh, leaders of the social democratic Bund, or union of Jewish workers, which was powerful before the 1917 revolution in Russia and remained a major force afterwards in Poland. Alter and Erlykh both died at the hands of Stalin's secret police during World War II: their executions set off an uproar in the democratic countries when, although Jewish, they were accused by Moscow of being Nazi spies. The mission of the J.A.F.C. was to publicize German atrocities against Jews on the Eastern Front and rally Jewish support for the Russian contribution to the Allied war effort.

51

Ten years later, the 1952 trial capped a period of anti-Jewish persecutions that began in Russia almost immediately after the foundation of the state of Israel in 1948. The defendants included Committee head and former Soviet labor leader Solomon Dridzo, known as Lozovsky, the Yiddish writers Itzik Feffer, Peretz Markish, David Bergelson, David Hofstein, and Leib Kvitko, Dr. Boris Shimeliovich, and union functionary I.S. Yusefovich, among others.

One excruciating feature of the book is Shimeliovich's description of his torture by Soviet secret police officers, in which he says he was physically struck 80 to 100 times per day during a two-month investigation in 1949. Revelations in the transcripts also include Lozovsky's courtroom accusation that "in the course of eight nocturnal interrogations... (the interrogator) Colonel Komarov repeated that I was, as a Jew, one of a lazy and dirty people, that all Jews were useless riffraff, that all opposition in the party based itself in the Jews, that Jews everywhere in the Soviet Union 'spit' on Soviet power, and that Jews hoped for the destruction of everything Russian."

The execution of the J.A.F.C. members in August 1952 was not made public in Russia and went unreported in the Western press, so the fate of the victims remained unknown until 1956, when six of Markish's poems were printed in the Moscow newspaper *Literaturnaya Gazeta*, setting off a public discussion of his mysterious fate. The full details of the executions remained undisclosed for some time afterward.

But while the destinies of Markish, Feffer, Bergelson, and other Soviet Yiddish cultural figures have thus been known and recounted for decades, Lozovsky has been largely forgotten. As noted by Louis Rapaport in his *Stalin's War Against the Jews*, Lozovsky was the highest Soviet official in the J.A.F.C. Indeed, later Soviet leader Nikita Khrushchev, who denounced Stalin's crimes, referred to the body as "the Lozovsky Committee."

One of a handful of prominent revolutionaries from 1917 to survive the main purges of the 1930s, Lozovsky was born Solomon A. Dridzo in 1878, the son of a teacher. He worked as a blacksmith before attending a series of schools, including a military academy where he was first introduced to socialist literature. He joined the Russian Social Democratic Labor Party in 1901, before it split between the Mensheviks and Bolsheviks.

In 1903, he was arrested for the first time by the tsarist authorities. He was a Bolshevik in the failed revolution of 1905, and was arrested in 1903 and exiled to Irkutsk in Siberia, but escaped to Europe. From 1909 to 1917 he lived in Geneva and Paris, joining the French socialist party and leading a union of hatmakers in Paris. He was an active contributor to journals edited by Leon Trotsky and Yuli Martov, as a member of a small faction standing between the moderate Mensheviks and the extremist and authoritarian Bolsheviks.

Lozovsky returned to Russia to participate in the Bolshevik revolution, and emerged as an articulate opponent of the new one-party state. Indeed, he briefly led his own small party that criticized the Bolshevik monopoly on power. As one of the few Russian Marxists with extensive Western political experience, however, he became a major figure in international radicalism as a head of the Red International of Labor Unions (R.I.L.U.), a federation of Communist entities that split off from the worldwide trade union movement to serve as a union arm of the Communist International.

Although it never attracted more than a handful of real unionists, mainly anarchosyndicalists from countries like Spain, the R.I.L.U. was a factor in global labor politics during the 1920s and 1930s. Its chief exploit was to recruit and direct an international network of clandestine couriers, ultimately under Soviet secret police control, using merchant seamen from pre-Hitler Germany, Scandinavia, the U.S., and other maritime countries.(1) The R.I.L.U. was dissolved in the 1930s by Stalin as a concession to Western social democratic labor leaders. Lozovsky's last hurrah was his work for the J.A.F.C. in World War II.

–Forward, July 7, 1995

Stalin's Forgotten Zion: A Review

(Stalin's Forgotten Zion, Birobidzhan and the Making of a Soviet Jewish Homeland, By Robert Weinberg with an introduction by Zvi Gitelman; photographs edited by Bradley Berman, University of California Press)

---

(1) On the international network of clandestine maritime couriers, the reader is directed to the author's *"Brotherhood of the Sea"*, New Brunswick, Transaction Books, 1986.

This is a profoundly disturbing book.

In May 1934, more than a year after Adolf Hitler's accession to power in Germany, Joseph Stalin's regime officially set up a Jewish Autonomous Region in the distant and desolate wastes of Siberia.

The Autonomous Region, named Birobidzhan after two tributaries of the Amur River, was mapped out along the Russo-Chinese border as a giant ghetto in which millions of Soviet Jews were to be resettled.

The area was first designated as an official Jewish area in 1928, the year Stalin triumphed over the Bolshevik Party opposition, which was chiefly led by the Jewish-born but non-observant Leon Trotsky, Lev Kamenev and Grigory Zinoviev.

Birobidzhan was soon labelled the Communist Zion, a Soviet alternative to the colonization movement then growing in Palestine.

The Palestine experiment, which resulted in the establishment of Israel 50 years ago, succeeded, while Birobidzhan fell into such complete obscurity that most people who encounter this book may be amazed to learn it even existed.

At the time the Autonomous Region was set up, the Birobidzhan district was mainly inhabited by Siberian Slavs, Mongols and immigrant Koreans. Its Jewish population never reached more than 20 percent, even though it was declared to be a Jewish political unit. Its economy never developed beyond primitive lumber cutting, and for several decades it was neglected by Moscow.

Throughout its history, Birobidzhan felt ripples of the ferocious human and cultural purges carried out by Stalin and his successors thousands of miles away. Yiddish books were burned in the region and political leaders "disappeared."

Since communism's collapse, the Jewish Autonomous Region has survived, after a fashion, as an administrative component of the Russian Federation. Although Jews today make up no more than 5 percent of its population, limited attempts at cultural and religious revival are now taking place.

But the events of its history are not what is disturbing in this book. Rather, it is the shocking equanimity with which its author, Robert Weinberg, has chosen to treat the overall topic of the "Soviet Jewish homeland." In reality, the better comparison to Birobidzhan is not with Israel but with Auschwitz. Stalin was no less a Jew-hater than

Hitler, and his intention in creating a super-ghetto in the Far East was hardly more benevolent than the Nazi "final solution."

The extent of Stalin's anti-Semitism has been established by a series of recent books. Even Weinberg admits (as if it were an afterthought or footnote) that Russian Jews themselves, in contrast with Western fellow-travelers, considered Birobidzhan a horrible hoax.

Stalin intended to kill them all. He failed to do so only because of the inherent inefficiency of Soviet genocidal practices when applied to large ethnic groups such as the Jews and Ukrainians, who numbered in the millions. Although an artificially created Soviet famine took millions of Christian and Jewish lives in Ukraine, Stalin could not, in the words of Nikita Khrushchev, fulfil his dream of deporting all Ukrainians to Siberia; "there were too many of them." His murderous policies were more effective against smaller groups, such as the Chechens and Ingushes, Meskhetians, Balkars, Karachais – all of them inhabitants of the Caucasus; Kalmyks, Crimean Tatars, Volga Germans, and Soviet Greeks, Kurds, and Koreans. These entire nations and ethnic groups were rounded up and deported to Central Asia en masse, during World War II. Stalin's repression was especially devastating when applied to individuals, families, and classes leading a more atomised existence, such as Trotskyists, Communist Party cadres in general, so-called "kulaks," etc.

But no mistake should be made: Birobidzhan was intended as a place for the forcible deportation and ultimate liquidation of Soviet Jews. Yet this book is suffused with the assumption that Stalin sincerely wished to create a homeland for the Jewish people and that Birobidzhan's "failure" – the fact that it did not become a super-ghetto – reflected an unrealistic but valid ideal.

A reader of this volume would never imagine that before the Communist seizure of power in 1917 the majority of Jewish socialists in Russia were Mensheviks who fiercely opposed the Bolshevik order. In this book, Jewish radicalism in Russia begins neither with the Mensheviks nor with the Jewish Bolsheviks like Trotsky, but with Birobidzhan, i.e. with Stalin.

Further, the book is repellent in its handling of the Communist suppression of religious Judaism. Weinberg comments disingenuously, "Given the absence of a synagogue and the prevailing political climate, which made open religious observance risky, the antireligious campaigns enjoyed no small degree of success as Jews found it difficult to practice their religion."

Really? What lurks behind the anodyne phrase "the prevailing political climate?" Would such polite language appear in a respectable publication about Jews in Nazi Germany? Later on, Weinberg observes that "with characteristic ambivalence," Communist officials expressed alarm when as many as 500 people, including military and police officers in uniform, attended High Holiday services in Birobidzhan in 1947. The next year, he notes without emphasis, official membership in the Jewish religious community of the region had dropped from 300 to 43.

Describing as "ambivalence" the fanatical commitment of Soviet Communists to the eradication of Jewish religious life is bad enough, but it is in the numbers that the real failure of the author becomes visible. This book attributes a decline of five-sixths in a religious community's membership in a single year to resignations and withdrawal from public affiliation. Weinberg never addresses the probability that more than a few of these were subjected to that well-known Soviet legal doctrine, "arrest, try, shoot."

Weinberg has been pilloried as a Stalin revisionist specifically because he has attempted to explain away statistics indicating mass liquidations. These statistics have been the subject of debates in the most authoritative academic journal in this field.

Such oversights become even more distressing when Weinberg touches on closer ground, namely Southern California. A caption states without elaboration, "In 1936 a delegation from Los Angeles went to (Birobidzhan) to present this souvenir pamphlet... The fate of the delegation is unknown." What kind of historian, writing in a publication of the University of California, would not seek at least to identify these Angelenos, who may have perished in the GuLag?

The collective memory of Weinberg and others associated with this project seems to be filled with such holes. We are told by the introduction's author, Zvi Gitelman, that "in the 1980s 'glasnost' revealed the failures of the system."

Strangely enough, the majority of Jews worldwide believe the struggle of the "refuseniks," Jewish dissidents refused permission to emigrate in the 1960s, the massacre of Jewish intellectuals in the early 1950s, the Hitler-Stalin pact and the great purges that preceded these horrors thoroughly "revealed the failures of the system."

At the end of his narrative, Weinberg claims bizarrely that "the fact that (Birobidzhan) had retained its official status for fifty years prepared the ground for the revival of Jewish life with the ascendance to power of Mikhail Gorbachev in the mid-1980s." Once again, the "refuseniks," the brave Lubavitch rabbis who smuggled in *matzot*, the defenders of a forbidden Hebrew education played no role; the revival came from Gorbachev, just as, 50 years before, Jewish radicalism putatively began with Stalin.

This is a treatment by and for people who refused to accept the truth about Soviet communism until it collapsed, and who still do not want to believe how evil it was. Had it been labelled more accurately as a denial of the Soviet Holocaust, it might never have seen print.

−San Francisco Chronicle, May 31, 1998

* * * * *

Chapter IV:

COMMUNISM IN AMERICA

Moscow Stooges Unmasked

A new compilation of documents released from Moscow's official files should end once and for all a debate that has divided American historians, and preoccupied American political discussion, since the 1930s: Was the American Communist Party a legitimate outgrowth of domestic radical traditions or a coldly manipulated tool of Soviet intelligence? *The Secret World of American Communism* by Harvey Klehr, John Earl Haynes and Fridrikh Igorevich Firsov shows inarguably that the C.P.U.S.A. was a stooge operation for Moscow.

Until the 1960s, historians never doubted Moscow's control over the American Communist Party. But with the rise of the "new history" during the Vietnam War, younger American academics began thinking of the party as a down-home, "people's front" affair practically independent of Soviet domination and only mildly Stalinist in outlook.

The evidence presented here is devastating to the theory of American party autonomy. These documents show that the party's leaders held Soviet secret police posts; maintained an illegal underground apparatus; encouraged members to spy on each other as well as on Trotskyists and other unorthodox leftists; sent its members for military, espionage and terror training in Russia, and performed many other clandestine tasks for its Soviet masters. While demonstrating for racial equality or pursuing other authentically progressive goals, the American Communists trembled at any sign of Kremlin disfavour and leapt to satisfy every demand made by the bosses of the K.G.B.'s predecessors, the O.G.P.U. and N.K.V.D. – including espionage.

The documents in this volume were selected from the Moscow archives of the U.S. party – maintained by the Russian government – and from the archives of the Communist International, or Comintern. The research was led by Mr. Klehr, a professor at Emory University in Atlanta. This new evidence massively confirms the position Mr. Klehr supported in 1984 in his book *The Heyday of American Communism.*

It also provides welcome support for similar documentation of Soviet infiltration already available.

For example, Benjamin Gitlow and Theodore Draper had previously published authoritative accounts based on direct observation of Soviet control over the C.P.U.S.A. In the radical '30s, such control was accepted as part of world revolution on the march. In the neo-radical '60s and progressive '70s, however, the party and its friends publicly denied it. Indeed, the entire communist effort in America was recast then, retroactively, to conform with the enlightened liberalism of the day. Only Neanderthal red-baiters, it was thought, could believe that the "heroic" radicals of the '30s were intentionally serving Stalin's dictatorship. The great value of *The Secret World of American Communism* is that it offers a definitive refutation of this view.

That said, it must be admitted that this book is something of a grab bag, assembling random elements, including a few that are not exactly earthshaking. (We learn, for instance, that one communist courier broke up with his wife, who was a "gold-digger.") Even so, there are many telling documents. Most shocking are those showing American communist misdeeds during the Spanish Civil War. The book also documents Soviet penetration of the atomic-bomb project at Los Alamos, and influence over a well-known correspondent for *The Christian Science Monitor*, Edmund Stevens.

The book resuscitates the case of Elizabeth Bentley, a former Russian spy in 1940s Washington who has been routinely trashed since then by leftist historians because of her revelations about communist infiltration of the Roosevelt administration. The book offers proof that Bentley's information was correct. It also confirms much that Whittaker Chambers said about the same subject, although the name of Alger Hiss, the main individual Chambers accused, does not appear.

The editors emphasize the secrecy of the communist movement, and rightly so. Communism was, after all, an international revolutionary conspiracy, in which secrecy was to be expected. Reputable past historians never overlooked this fact, but it has been lost in the general cultural discussion of 1930s radicalism, which has in most cases entailed an excessive naïveté – or wilful ignorance – about the true nature of communist activity. This naïveté has been especially pronounced among academics, whose first concern was often to avoid any point of view that might open them up to charges of McCarthyism. A great deal of intellectual dishonesty was the result.

It is true that the American party never played more than a small part in the history of international communism. It was only briefly and rarely a true mass movement, mainly in New York and on the West Coast during the 1930s. But its legacy is still with us, most notably in the intellectual culture, where anti-anticommunism is still the reigning orthodoxy. Soviet communism remains one of the great historical issues of the 20th century, and our attitudes toward it tell us a great deal about ourselves. It is not necessary to go all the way to Moscow to understand this particular issue, but it certainly helps.

–The Wall Street Journal, April 20, 1995

The *Collected Works* of John Reed

An icon of the radical left, once played weirdly on screen by Warren Beatty in *Reds*, John Reed is now hardly known as an author. This collection is an attempt to bring him back into vogue with the three books Reed published in his lifetime: *Insurgent Mexico* (1914), *The War in Eastern Europe* (1916), and *Ten Days That Shook the World* (1919), the latter on which *Reds* was based. It is a triumph more of politics than of literature.

Reed was born in Portland, Oregon, in 1887, to a rich family. After graduating from Harvard University, he entered the Bohemian life of Greenwich Village in Manhattan, writing mainly for magazines, while frequenting poetry salons. He was swept into radicalism when he reported on a strike led by the Industrial Workers of the World [the "Wobblies"] in the silk mills of Paterson, New Jersey. He went to Mexico, where a revolution was in full swing. Bankrolled by Moscow to the tune of a million roubles [according to *The Secret World of American Communism*], he would become a founder of America's pathetic Communist Party.

Of the three volumes reprinted here, *Insurgent Mexico* reads the best today. While it's clear he never fully mastered Spanish, Reed described with relish the Texas-Mexico border, with stage cowboys and sheriffs on one side, and, on the other, assorted Wild Bunch-style rebels who broke into song and cut rodeo tricks when not shooting unarmed prisoners. The book's idiom recalls a long lost time when American radicalism and the frontier seemed to go together. When Reed crosses the border southward, and joins a *tropa*, or party of soldiers, a narrative emerges without great social or political insight, but filled with a love of landscape and of masculine adventure. Reed displayed a Breughelian talent for detail, picking out, for example, a colour bearer in Pancho Villa's ranks who, asked the goal of the revolutionary war, says, "Why, it is good, fighting. You don't have to work in the mines!"

The obvious flaw in Reed's own approach to Mexico remains its overt sentimentality. All the time, he insisted he was a correspondent, not a soldier, but his passionate advocacy would be viewed with deep suspicion today. Or at least so one hopes; foreign reporters, in the style of the infamous Pilger and Dimbleby, still seem inordinately prone to recycling propaganda once they reach exotic climes. Reed writes romantically even of Villa's murders and other atrocities for which – given his enthusiasm for the revolutionary cause – Reed himself may be considered an accomplice.

This sentimentalism was not unique to Reed. As a journalist, he was a late exemplar of the fin-de-siècle tradition of vivid reporting filtered through a literary sensitivity. He was attuned, above all, to the poetic nature of his subjects. His writing on the Mexican Revolution is interspersed with translations of *corridos* – popular ballads on the great events of the time – which remain quite affecting. But unlike the majority of his counterparts, Reed was exceptionally susceptible to political intoxication – indeed, his case was so severe he may be considered the outstanding specimen of the syndrome.

This approach served him poorly when he turned his pen to the Eastern Front during World War I, in *The War in Eastern Europe*. Remarkably enough, Reed proves an early and extreme partisan of Serbian ultranationalism, in its most absurd and violent forms. Reed's comments on Serbian radicalism assumed a hallucinatory form that has once again become familiar. Croatia, Bosnia, even Slovenia, all were inhabited by "Serbian peoples," destined, according to Reed, to be united in "an empire fifteen millions strong... which will liberate the energies of the fighting, administrative [sic] people of the kingdom of Serbia, penned in their narrow mountain valleys, to the exploitation of the rich plains country, and the powerful life of ships at sea."

Reed was notably given to ugly stereotypes, occasionally dipping into broad characterizations about Mexican morals. In writing about Eastern Europe, he repeated uncritically many opinions that even then were considered disreputable. The Albanians, he claimed, were a people imported from the Caucasus (a Serb fantasy). The Romanians were "Italianised gypsies," a viewpoint lately resurrected by no less a personage than Vladimir Zhirinovsky. But Reed adds his own doses of venom: Poles were "the ugliest race in the world," and there is much about Jews in Reed's Mexican and East European reportage that would not today be put in print if produced fresh. But in a collection of this sort, it can hardly be left out.

Reed turned his experience in the Bolshevik coup of October 1917 into a classic of "faction" *avant la lettre*. His *Ten Days That Shook the World* appeared with a preface by Lenin himself – who praised Reed's account as "truthful." (Lenin, in fact, has the sole blurb appearing on this edition's dustjacket.) *Ten Days* is one of a number of books (others include Brecht's plays and poems, and Malraux's *Man's Fate*) that destroyed generations of young intellectuals – morally in the West, physically under Soviet and fascist dictatorships – by leading them into the most extreme, nihilist forms of self sacrifice in the name of Communism. It is still a riveting read, which is precisely the problem. Having first devoured it as a teenager, I well remember the excitement it conveyed, in its moment-by-moment account of the inexorable drive of Lenin and his Bolsheviks to power.

Who, having read them, can easily forget Reed's bullet-like words? "In the rain, the bitter chill, the great throbbing city [St. Petersburg, then Petrograd] under grey skies was rushing faster and faster toward – what?" The next chapter begins grimly: "In the relations of a weak government and rebellious people there comes a time when every act of the authorities exasperates the masses, and every refusal to act excites their contempt."

This Leninist epic now appears to us with its seams and stitches obvious. It was published two years after the events it describes, and much of it was derived not from Reed's own observation but from newspapers. Some of it is shocking to contemplate today, as when Reed happily quotes the Bolshevik Lev Karakhan's description of the new regime: "A loose organization, sensitive to the popular will as expressed through the Soviets, allowing local forces full play... The initiative of the new society shall come from below." By the time *Ten Days* was printed, it was obvious to all, even acolytes of Bolshevism like Reed, that this was nonsense.

Karakhan, later a distinguished Soviet diplomat, was murdered by Stalin in the purges, like virtually all the other Bolshevik leaders mentioned in Reed's book (with the obvious exceptions being Lenin and Stalin, the latter of who plays almost no role.) Indeed, for many years the chief importance of *Ten Days* for Communist studies – both inside the former Soviet Union and abroad – resided in its pre-Stalin record of the actions of Trotsky, Grigory Zinoviev, Lev Kamenev, V.A. Antonov-Ovseyenko, D.B Ryazanov, Aleksei Rykov, Aleksandr Shlyapnikov, Nikolai Krylenko, P.E. Dybenko – the heroes of October who went from the heights of revolutionary power to obscure and brutal ends within twenty years, names once acclaimed and then erased from history.

This edition has many flaws beyond those of Reed himself. It would have been interesting to read some of his labour journalism and related pieces written on the American scene, and the inexplicable failure to include that work – probably a function of editorial laziness – belies the volume's claim to be a "collected works."

Finally, Robert A. Rosenstone, a mediocre liberal/leftist biographer of Reed, has written an introduction that is no more than a brief hagiography of Reed the Communist Saint. That Rosenstone declares *Ten Days* Reed's "most American" book speaks for itself, and badly; but recent American radical intellectuals love to indulge their penchant for provocative idiocies of that sort. *Ten Days* was taken up by the Communists not for its "American" qualities but because the author surrendered completely to the propagandist spirit. He was valuable to Moscow as an example of submission, not of enterprise.

Nowhere does Rosenstone see fit to discuss Reed's lover, Louise Bryant. Also unmentioned is Boardman Robinson, illustrator of the radical organ *The Masses*, and creator of an artistic accompaniment to Reed's East European reportage more attractive in some ways than Reed's own writing. Robinson was an artist of real talent who today is unjustifiably neglected. Worse, Rosenstone omits any doubts expressed about the Bolshevik revolution by other American radicals

Reed encountered in Russia. The anti-Bolshevik dissent of Emma Goldman and others of Reed's contemporaries was included even in *Reds*, making Hollywood, paradoxically enough, truer to fact than the Modern Library, publisher of this volume.

Most importantly, Rosenstone ignores all mention of Reed's ambiguous death. The best judgment on John Reed remains that delivered by an authentic revolutionary who never bowed to Leninism, the anarchist Alexander Berkman. The companion of Emma Goldman, Berkman was imprisoned in America for many years for an act of pro-labour terrorism, and deported to Russian in 1919. Unlike Reed, Berkman set down what he saw and published it without redecoration. Describing the funeral in October 1920 of the 33-year-old Reed, Berkman wrote in his book *The Bolshevik Myth*, "A fresh grave along the Kremlin wall, opposite the Red Square, the honoured resting place of the revolutionary martyrs. I stand at the brink, supporting Louise Bryant who has entirely abandoned herself to grief. She had hastened from America to meet Jack after a long separation. Missing him in Petrograd, she proceeded to Moscow only to learn that Reed had been ordered to Baku to the Congress of Eastern Peoples… [H]e was unwilling to undertake the arduous journey. But Zinoviev insisted… and like a good Party soldier Jack obeyed. But his weakened constitution could not withstand the hardships of Russian travel and its fatal infections."

In October 1993, Moscow mayor Yuri Luzhkov called for removal of all the Communist corpses, Lenin's and Reed's included, from Red Square, and their reburial elsewhere.

–The American Spectator, July 1995

Poseur Poser: Tina Modotti

Tina Modotti (1896-1942), Hilton Kramer wrote in The *New York Times,* was once known as "Edward Weston's mistress and model during his crucial Mexican period, [who] was also an accomplished, if minor, photographer in her own right." Today, however, she is probably better known than Weston, at least in the universities.

Born in Italy, raised in San Francisco, and morally tarnished if not murdered in Mexico, Tina Modotti has become an icon of the academic left: a kind of junior partner to Frida Kahlo. Unlike Kahlo, she does not bear the cachet of physical handicaps or such extra assets, for a representative of the fabled "other," as Kahlo's Jewish background. But Modotti has an item in her biography that has made her as appealing to academically-tenured revolutionary fantasists: Modotti was a full time functionary of the Stalinist movement during the 1930s.

No amount of campus- or museum-based idolatry can promote Modotti's art above the "minor" level identified by Mr. Kramer. Still it is useful to study the life of Tina Modotti because she stands as perhaps the best representative of all those personalities of the 1930s whose ideals, for those who truly possessed them, were betrayed, and whose lives were ruined by Stalinism. Two recent books – *Shadows, Fire, Snow: The Life of Tina Modotti*, by Patricia Albers, and Pino Cacucci's *Tina Modotti: A Life* – demonstrate the extent to which the Modotti cult has grown, while also showing the limitations of American publishing. Each book, in its own way, is an appalling product.

Patricia Albers' offering is by far the worst. Its author communicates her limitations in the opening pages; while describing Modotti's death, she writes that her heroine's "last flickering perceptions are of darkness, solitude, and drift." It is hard to prove such a claim wrong, but it would be interesting to have it sourced.

Mrs. Albers writes in only one mode: gushing enthusiasm. Every event in her book – which covers some of the most terrible episodes in 20th-century history – is treated as if it were a party with great refreshments and wonderful favours. Mrs. Albers brings to the story of Tina Modotti, art photographer and, as we learn, secret police agent, the sensibility of a suburban matron hosting a reception for a visiting feminist professor. This is, perhaps, appropriate, or at least authentic, in that Modotti has become an idol precisely to that elite class which, for three generations in the industrialized nations, has dealt with its neuroses by making up roles as Third World revolutionaries.

Mrs. Albers had the good fortune to locate a trunkload of papers held by the survivors of Modotti's early companion, the San Francisco artist Roubaix de L'Abrie Richey, nicknamed "Robo," and she has used these materials to pad the first third of her book. But the portrait she paints is an unwittingly unpleasant one, and the reader is fed with pompous generalities and clichés, often based on pure speculation.

Thus, we are told of the young Tina's reaction to Italian setbacks in World War I, "the military debacle had cut off communication with the family in Italy, leaving Tina, [her sister] Mercedes, and [her father] Giuseppe frantic with anxiety. Was Tina also experiencing guilt that she had been absorbed in [theatre] as her loved ones suffered? If so, it was not the last time she would anguish over the thought of art making in the face of human affliction."

Tina Modotti was a deceiver born, who, in her adolescence in the North Beach section of San Francisco, learned two dangerous things. One was that she as a good actress; the other was that such talents might be better turned to seducing and controlling friends and acquaintances than to pursuing a real stage career before audiences that knew they were audiences and that she was only acting.

For the rest of her life she acted out characters: as an aesthete, "Madame de Richey;" as the photographic assistant and disciple of Edward Weston, and as a Stalinist terrorist. She played each of these with sure instincts for the right gesture, consummate attention to detail, and, above all, an extravagant sense of drama. But each remained a role; she never matured beyond playacting. She was an aesthete when poses about the "Religion of Art and Beauty" were already discredited by the carnage of the First World War. She was a photographer who never grew beyond imitation of Weston.

And while she claimed, with her Stalinist peers, to be a proletarian revolutionary, she was mainly a bureaucrat, although a homicidal one. But, of course, it might also be said that the Stalinist Communists only played at revolution, and that the intellectuals who flocked to it were all, in one manner or another, poseurs; with, unfortunately, the power of life and death over those they disliked.

The depiction of Modotti's early relationship with the distinctly weedy Robo Richey is drenched with the aesthetic posturing to which they both surrendered themselves. This was a pose that, at the time they assumed it, in the late 1910s, was already overripe. Some twenty five years had passed since the heyday of the great San Francisco artistic rebels – "Les Jeunes," which included the typographer Porter Garnett, the versifier Gelett Burgess, and the essayist and novelist Frank Norris – but Modotti and Robo acted as if *The Yellow Book* had just hit the stands and Oscar Wilde were about to drop in for dinner.

After Modotti has written her tenth or twentieth letter to Weston offering him rose petals and acclaiming the beauty he has brought into her life, one really wishes she, rather than Frida Kahlo, had been hit by a streetcar. But Modotti was soon to move from her delirious aesthetic self-indulgence to the Stalinist nightmare of the political will to power.

She went to Mexico, first with Richey but later with Weston, whom she had met while working as a model. Weston taught her to take photographs, but her early productions were undistinguished. We are told that Richey published drawings in *Gale's Magazine,* a radical journal issued in Mexico City, but research on such a topic, which might have produced a valuable contribution, is too much for Mrs. Albers. Instead she coos, "the pair relished the bravado of seeing Robo's signature on the cover of a Communist magazine during the period of the so-called Red Scare, when U.S. Attorney General A. Mitchell Palmer was unleashing raids on suspected radicals." But this is mere boilerplate; it didn't take all that much bravado to publish such stuff in revolutionary Mexico, when Palmer's writ only ran north of the Rio Grande, and when *Gale's Magazine* was largely unknown and unread.

Richey died of smallpox in Mexico, leaving Modotti to commandeer Weston's salon, already dominated by Communist intellectuals, and which thanks to her soon including the American Soviet agents Bertram and Ella Wolfe. This circle included the prominent artists Diego Rivera and David Siqueiros. Modotti attached herself to Rivera as well as Frida Kahlo. Modotti also joined a Mexican neo-futurist avant garde group, Los Estridentistas. And, influenced as much by their interest in technological images as by the revolutionary chatter swirling around her, Modotti began producing "modernist" photographs of an openly propagandist character.

She was following fads, without evincing real artistic strength: she went easily from portraits of Weston, still posing in the manner of a turn of the century dandy, to floral studies, to stagey images of workers and peasants in struggle. The latter fascination, however, led to her involvement with one of the most shocking events in the history of Stalinism: the assassination of Julio Antonio Mella, a Cuban Communist whose real name was Nicanor McPartland. Mella was Modotti's lover. He was not her first sexual-political attachment as she had already been the lover of one of Stalin's most vicious terrorists: a shark-like fellow-Italian named Vittorio Vidali.

Even today, the killing of Mella remains an unhealed wound, exemplary of the impact of Stalinism. Mella had gone into exile in Mexico after a flamboyant career leading the revolutionary opposition to the Cuban dictator Gerardo Machado. Mella had become a prominent Communist but was sympathetic to Trotsky, a quote from whom appears on the sheet in his typewriter in a famous photograph of the machine taken by Modotti. That photograph (*Mella's Typewriter*, or *La Técnica*, 1928) appears as an illustration in Mrs. Albers' book, without elucidation.

Mella was shot on January 10, 1929, while walking with Modotti, who was clinging to him. The bullets passed through him but missed her, exciting the suspicion of Mexican detectives. During the ensuing investigation, she demonstrated her theatrical talents to the maximum. Photographs taken in the aftermath of the crime show her transformed from the determined, dominating personality visible in her "family pictures" with Richey and in Weston's portraits into a trembling, naïve child-woman. Rivera and others declared that Mella had been killed on orders from Machado, and the Mexican police cleared Modotti of involvement. But intraparty Communist gossip, from the moment of Mella's death to the present, has insisted that Mella was killed for his Trotskyism – the first individual in the world to be executed for that infraction.

Mella became a deathless symbol of Communism in Latin America, definitely worth more dead than he would have been had he remained alive, and the controversy over his murder has been especially troublesome in Cuba. With the conquest of power in 1959 by Castro's radicals, whose relations with Cuba's old official Communists were rocky at best, it was widely expected that the Machado government archives would be opened and the debate settled forever. But no such disclosure occurred.

The conflicting versions of the Mella affair were revived early in 1999, on the 70th anniversary of the assassination. A considerable quarrel erupted on H-DIPLO, an internet discussion group on diplomatic history administered at Michigan State University. Cuban functionaries strove mightily to deny any claims that Mella might have fallen foul of Stalinist orthodoxy. In a typical comment, Carlos Alzúgaray, a high official with Cuba's Ministry of Foreign Affairs, wrote, "If it is of course essentially pernicious that 'official' history prevails in a country, it is also counterproductive and non-historiographical [sic] to adopt the exact opposite position. By the way, I am sure it is not only Cuba or the Soviet Union and the former socialist countries where 'official' history is practiced."

This discussion, if it may be called that, went on for some time until the entry into it of a Russian historian, Viktor Kheifets, who had access to the Moscow archives. Kheifets demonstrated that, although the Cuban officials still denied it, seven decades later, Mella had been expelled from the party. But the Russian historian also opined that final blame in his death could not be assigned. He wrote, "Machado's motive to kill Mella was strong enough… however, the case isn't proven yet…If we want to find the direct proofs of Machado's responsibility, Cuban archives in Havana should be checked once more." Yet these sources remain padlocked under Castro's rule.

The Mella case is only one in a fairly long list of unresolved deaths of Communist dissidents outside the Soviet Union. Nevertheless, regardless of the obstacles to a final clarification of the Mella affair, one thing is sure: after it, Tina Modotti committed herself, willingly or otherwise, to the clandestine Stalinist apparatus for the rest of her days. And she never again publicly, or in secret Communist documents, alluded to Julio Antonio Mella.

Modotti was deported from Mexico in 1930, to a Germany in which the Communist movement was then powerful. Vidali, the sinister secret police agent, became her permanent companion and seeming protector. The next twelve years saw the eventual abandonment of photography as she graduated to propagandistic writing and then to administrative responsibilities in Russia itself, leavened by secret courier assignments abroad. She was recruited to work in the so-called International Defence for Class War Prisoners, known in the U.S. as the International Labour Defence. This body controlled a money laundering and political espionage network of considerable extent and effectiveness. Characteristically, Mrs. Albers handles this reality with a chirpy, upbeat tone.

Mrs. Albers is equally problematic in dealing with the horrors of Stalinism. She baldly states certain facts: that the assassination of Soviet number two Sergei Kirov, in 1934, led to "years of monstrous carnage and terror;" that Vidali and Modotti themselves fell under suspicion; that during the Spanish civil war, in which Vidali was a prominent figure, the anti-Stalinist Andreu Nin, head of the Partit Obrer d'Unificació Marxista (P.O.U.M.) was kidnapped, tortured, and murdered by Stalinist agents. She even points out that Modotti was involved in the murder of a dissident Communist who had come from Brazil to fight in the Moscow-controlled International Brigades, Alberto Bomilcar Besouchet. Besouchet's death came about only because he had been associated with the Brazilian singer Elsie Houston, who was the ex-wife of the French surrealist and Trotskyist poet Benjamin Péret. Péret was also in Spain, and like George Orwell, barely escaped Stalin's henchmen.

Yet as devastating as such revelations should prove to those who idealize Modotti and other 1930s Communists, Mrs. Albers remains largely unmoved. "Tina most likely never set eyes on Alberto Bomilcar Besouchet," Mrs. Albers writes. "Blinded by tyrannical self-discipline, desperation to win the war, and a belief in the value of correct ideology, the woman who braved hails of gunfire to save children's lives sacrificed Alberto Besouchet (and no doubt others) for what she believed to be the good of the cause."

From this point onward, the narrative assumes a rather sombre cast. For Mrs. Albers it is all merely a tragic end to a life of festivities; and indeed, the fall of the Spanish Republic in 1939, made inevitable by Stalin's aggressive drive for control of the Loyalist side, saw considerable tragedy. Modotti and Vidali escaped to Mexico. But Modotti's time was short, very likely because the best description for her situation is an old cliché: she knew too much. On January 5, 1942, she attended a party at the home of a prominent German Communist exile. Late that night, she took a taxi home, but arrived at a hospital instead. There she died. The medical report listed the cause of her death as a heart attack. Almost immediately, the rumours that circulated at the time of Mella's death were repeated; this time Vidali, who did not attend the funeral, was accused by some of her elimination. Mrs. Albers refuses to examine this possibility at length, writing that such charges "are buttressed only by conjecture and circumstantial evidence."

The author of the second recent book on Modotti, Pino Cacucci, a convinced anti-Stalinist, goes further: he notes that, in the similar death of the anti-Stalinist Victor Serge, the victim's friends in Mexico City "maintained that in the 1940s the [local union] of taxi drivers was controlled by the Communist Party, which had used them to keep order at demonstrations and to carry out punitive missions." This charge is supported by the Venona decryptions of Soviet secret police communications.

Cacucci's book could have provided an excellent antidote to the weaknesses of Mrs. Albers, were it not disfigured in other ways. Put simply, his book, which originally appeared in Italian, was assassinated in English by inept translation and a complete lack of fact checking. To list all the misspelled names, misattributed facts, and other mistakes in the American edition of his work would require a separate essay. But Cacucci, at least, understands the full horror of Modotti's life, a life to devoted to power over others, in which ideals, if present at all, accounted for very, very little.

–*The New Criterion, October 1999*

Political Murder: The Carlo Tresca Case

Dorothy Gallagher's *All the Right Enemies: The Life and Murder of Carlo Tresca* presents one of the most remarkable personalities in 20th century American history: an Italian-born labour leader of anarchist convictions, a pronounced anti-Stalinist, who was assassinated in 1943, very possibly at the instance of the Communist Party. The Tresca case has been discussed for decades by veterans of the 1930s dissident left – anarchists, Lovestoneites, Trotskyists – as well as by aged Italian-Americans and a handful of historical scholars. That a book such as this has been published, and, although written from a leftist viewpoint, that it should be accurate in its assessment of Soviet political terrorism in the West during the period, seems a miracle: a small and flawed one, but a miracle nonetheless.

The character of Carlo Tresca is inseparable from the labour culture of this first half of the 20th century, with its deep idealism and spirit of self-sacrifice, and its genuinely religious attachment to the redemptionist doctrines of anarchism and socialism. His background was, unsurprisingly, middle-class. What is rather more surprising is that he did not, like so many petit-bourgeois rebels of the time, turn his back on university and guild and launch himself into the revolu-

tionary movement at a precocious age. Rather, he trained profession-
ally as an accountant, and, had he stayed in Italy, might well have
remained an obscure figure in the vastness of Italian radicalism.

Tresca came into his own once he arrived in the United States in
1904, at the age of twenty-five, in flight from a political trial in Italy.
(His brother, who preceded him in going to America, had established
a medical practice.) He was soon editing an Italian-language newspaper in Philadelphia, with the characteristic title *Il Proletario*.

Tresca's declared enemies, in addition to the normal anarchist
gallery of demons ranging from priests to bankers, included the Italian
padrone who preyed on recent immigrants, extorting their meagre capital in exchange for jobs, and the Italian criminal gangs, predecessors
of the Mafia, who enacted similar roles as loan sharks. He soon attracted protest from Italian diplomatic officials in the United States as well
as the unfriendly attentions of the federal postal service, which began
barring issues of his periodicals from the mails.

By 1912 Carlo Tresca had become famous in the world of
American labour radicalism; in that year he was ushered into the full
glare of publicity by the celebrated textile workers' strike in Lawrence,
Massachusetts, called by the anarchosyndicalist Industrial Workers of
the World (IWW), or "Wobblies." William Haywood, the former Rocky
Mountain mine organizer and spokesman for the IWW, had left
Lawrence under threat of indictment. With powerful oratorical and
publicity gifts, Tresca, who came to be called "the Bull of Lawrence,"
rallied the strikers. The entire spectacle profoundly moved labour and
liberal opinion throughout the nation.

For the next twenty-five years, until the middle of the 1930s, Tresca
carried out a unique function as the civic conscience of the community of poorer Italian newcomers to America, while becoming a popular figure as well in the Bohemian political and literary circles that
spawned individuals like John Reed. His enemies continued to include
the old symbols – the hypocritical priest, the parasitical gangster, but
in the 1920s and 1930s he acquired two new and deadlier ones,
Fascism and Communism.

Prior to his flight from Europe, Tresca had known Benito
Mussolini, then a young socialist radical. After Mussolini's accession
to power in 1922, Tresca, through a journal he had begun to publish
in 1917 called *Il Martello* (The Hammer), emerged as one of the most

articulate, effective, popular, and irritating voices of Italian antifas-
cism. Tresca early on exhibited a willingness to join with Moscow-line
Communists. But by the time of the Spanish civil war of 1936-39, if
not earlier, Tresca had learned that Soviet Communism represented
no less a menace to the cause he championed than Fascism.

The single event that seems to have pushed Tresca into active con-
demnation of the Soviet Union was the murder of the Italian anarchist writer Camillo Berneri in Republican Spain in 1937. Berneri was
the outstanding younger personality in Italian anarchism at the time,
known and beloved in the international anarchist movement, and
hounded from country to country by Mussolini's agents. Berneri was
kidnapped and killed during fighting that broke out in Barcelona
between anarchists and the dissident Communist Partit Obrer
d'Unificació Marxista (P.O.U.M.) on one side, and Soviet-controlled
police on the other. (This fighting is best described in George Orwell's
Homage to Catalonia.) At the time, the Stalinist purges in the U.S.S.R.
were at their height, and Tresca recognized the murder of Berneri as
an extension of the purge apparatus into the West.

Then, a year later, in 1938, a second case erupted in New York,
after Juliet Stuart Poyntz, a well-known Communist intellectual and
probable Soviet secret police agent, disappeared. Tresca and a small
group of active anti-Stalinists charged that Poyntz was another victim
of the Stalinist terror.

These affairs and the 1939 Stalin-Hitler pact drove Tresca into a
fury of opposition to the Soviets and their Communist supporters
around the world. But it was the entry of the U.S. into World War II,
with the U.S.S.R. cast as an ally in the struggle against fascism, that set
the stage for Tresca's murder. He was shot to death on January 11,
1943, at the corner of Fifth Avenue and 15th Street in Manhattan, a
year after the strange demise in Mexico City of the Italian-American
photographer and Soviet secret police functionary Tina Modotti. The
cases are, perhaps unsurprisingly, linked.

There is sufficient evidence, as thoroughly developed by Dorothy
Gallagher, to believe that the actual killer was Carmine (Lilo) Galante,
an associate of John Dioguardi (Johnny Dio), a notorious mobster.
Galante would later rise to the heights of Mafia power before being
spectacularly gunned down in a Brooklyn restaurant in 1979, thirty
six years after Tresca. The Galante assassination has its own folklore

73

– a photograph of the body, with a cigar clenched in its teeth, was widely reproduced in media, and one report held that an unknown man had walked up to spit on the corpse, remarking "That's for Carlo Tresca" before vanishing into the crowd.

From the beginning, however, there was speculation that the killer of Tresca, while owing a primary allegiance to the Mafia, was paid or otherwise guided by Soviet, Italian, or American Communists who sought the elimination of an eloquent opponent. At the time of his death, Tresca was preparing an issue of *Il Martello* replete with attacks on Stalinism. Speculation similarly surrounded the figure of another Italian political activist with whom Tresca had once been acquainted, none other than Vittorio Vidali, Soviet secret police mercenary par excellence and the lover of the ill-fated Modotti.

Tresca was killed just as he was organizing a major political fight to influence the United States government in its wartime dealings with Italy. The Fascist regime was in deep crisis, an Allied invasion was clearly on the agenda, and efforts were underway to coordinate the establishment of a post-Fascist government. These last were centered in Washington, in an entity titled the Italian-American Victory Council, set up under the authority of the federal Office of War Information. The Communists, vying for a leading role in postwar Italy, sought to participate in the Victory Council, but Tresca called for a close watch on these activities by the U.S. government. He also opposed involvement in the Victory Council of a New York Italian political boss with Fascist sympathies, the newspaper publisher Generoso Pope.

Galante was arrested in the case, but was released and never charged. Indeed, New York authorities never indicted anybody for the killing of Tresca, and to this day it remains officially unsolved. Miss Gallagher somewhat hesitantly concludes that the crime originated with the Mafia alone. But there remain curious coincidences that point to Communist-Mafia collaboration. One, which Miss Gallagher mentions without sufficient elaboration, is that two of the most notorious and extreme Stalinists in the history of American Communism, waterfront labour thug Frederick N. (Blackie) Myers and Soviet spy Louis Goldblatt, were suspiciously close to Galante on the night of the murder. Another, which she seemed not to know about, was that one Albert Marinelli, a New York politician with whom Johnny Dio and Lilo Galante were associated, had also been involved in a Soviet espionage and terror operation in the U.S. known as the "Robinson-Rubens" case.

Dorothy Gallagher's achievements in her book are two: she effectively recreated the atmosphere and attitudes of the Italian radical labour movement in America during the early 20th century, and she extensively researched certain accessible but neglected subjects. Thus, she recapitulated known details about the life of the frightful Vidali, including his decades-long, but unsuccessful attempt, while serving as a leading parliamentarian of the Italian Communist Party, to clear himself of the "Stalinist killer" label.

The drawbacks of *All the Right Enemies* consist of a number of gaps and errors – items like the death of Berneri and the Marinelli affair are left almost untouched, and Miss Gallagher is simply unfamiliar with some of the political history of the epoch – and an attitude, characteristic of many recent studies of radical movements, of moral neutrality between Soviet Communism and American capitalism.

Miss Gallagher, for example, equates the depredations of the Soviet secret police with the paranoid fantasies of American Left-liberals about "secret teams" of criminals in league with American intelligence authorities, and she closes with a slap at those who, sharing Tresca's radical background, eventually broke completely with the left and rallied to capitalist democracy in the face of the Communist betrayal of their ideals. Yet the truth is that such "apostates" have learned much better than today's left-wing historians the real lessons of the death of Carlo Tresca – and of millions more.

–Commentary, November 1988

He Ain't Worth a Lick: Paul Robeson

The years 1997-98 saw an international campaign to turn a man generally and deservedly forgotten into an African American hero. According to his advocates, the singer Paul Robeson, who would have turned 100 in 1998, deserves to join Martin Luther King, Jr. and W.E.B. DuBois as the subject of a United States postage stamp.

In December 1997, the Citizens Stamp Advisory Committee denied a request for a Robeson stamp, despite having received nearly 90,000 letters and signatures in support of it – in the end not that many, considering the size of the American population. The Committee refused to explain its decision. Then in April 1998, some sixty members of the U.S. Congress signed a letter calling on the Committee to reconsider. "Paul Robeson's contribution to American society and his personal accomplishments are to be extolled," the congressional letter read. "[He] is perhaps the only true Renaissance man the 20th century has known," the legislators opined, in a spectacular expression of American narcissism, philistinism, "political correctness," and Congressional silliness. "A scholar… lawyer… all-American athlete… classical musical and Broadway actor; vigorous opponent of racism and champion of human rights… best known for his grand baritone singing voice and his political activism."

New Jersey Representative Frank Pallone joined Black Panther veteran Bobby Rush, his Illinois colleague and fellow Democrat, in a House resolution urging the stamp issue. Rush predictably praised Robeson as "an advocate for the rights of African-American and other oppressed people" who "sacrificed his career as a world renowned singer and actor." In a printed statement, Pallone added, "There is no question that Paul Robeson deserves this long overdue recognition. Issuing a commemorative postage stamp is one way we can honour this great man."

Pallone's staff representative, Ted Loud, averred that his boss was mainly motivated by the coincidence of Robeson having graduated from Rutgers University, in Pallone's district. But Loud himself – in a breathtaking distortion of facts – described Robeson as "a pioneer of the [American] civil rights movement."

While the U.S. Postal Service has so far disappointed Robeson's supporters, other organizations have been more obliging. At the annual Grammy Awards in March 1998, the National Academy of Recording Arts and Sciences presented a posthumous lifetime achievement award to the singer. In April, the Bravo cable television channel broadcast "Paul Robeson: Tribute to An Artist," a 30-minute documentary. In the same month the New-York Historical Society announced an exhibition, "Paul Robeson: Bearer of a Culture," to kick off the work of more than 100 local memorial committees. One of dozens of Robeson centennial websites listed events around America and the world, ranging from "films, forum, celebration" at the Gene Autry Museum in

Los Angeles to an event in the International Labour Chorus Festival in Vaasa, Finland. *The New York Times* reported that Robeson enthusiasts include such establishment figures as David Rockefeller and Brooke Astor.

This is not simply another demand for belated recognition of a talented black. The pro-Robeson campaign represents the latest attempt to sell the American people a falsified, anti-anticommunist, upside down version of their history. The hoopla on Robeson's behalf has been especially vigorous in the San Francisco Bay Area, America's last redoubt of Soviet nostalgia. Much of the propaganda produced by the celebration committees is specially tailored to classroom use. For example, high school students in San Leandro, a working class suburb of San Francisco, heard a lecture by a self-anointed "historian" of Robeson's career, which soon was repeated to students at nearby California State University, Hayward. Both audiences were treated to the saga of how the Cold War "blighted" the great man's life. Yet there is much about this putative hero that his apologists typically fail to mention.

Robeson, who was born in Princeton, New Jersey in 1898 and died in Philadelphia in 1976, first became famous as an all-American football player at Rutgers, then gained renown as an actor and singer. His most notable performances were in plays and musicals that today tend to be condemned as racist: Shakespeare's *Othello*, Eugene O'Neill's *The Emperor Jones*, *Showboat* (where he sang "Ol' Man River"). His gifts were widely appreciated. *San Francisco Chronicle* critic Alfred Frankenstein, who was no sucker, wrote in December 1941 that Robeson had "the greatest bass voice in the world" and praised "the splendour of his tone and his commanding individuality." But Frankenstein also had this to say about Robeson's concert program: "I leave it to the oracles to figure out the political place of Communist fellow-travellers and fellow-traveller music in the present scheme of things... Hanns Eisler's 'Peat Bog Soldiers,' which is, or once was, an official Communist song, deals with the same rousing elements of rhythm and melody that may be found in any crowd music whether its shirt be red, brown, black, or khaki... The Municipal Chorus... had a grand time delivering the occasional spoken lines in dat good ol' down Souf tawk day lunned from deir good ol' Mammy in Alabam'."

It's interesting to note that the recent surge of publicity about

Robeson as a political figure has caused renewed interest in his music and films, rather than the way around. The man is being rehabilitated for his politics rather than his artistry.

During the 1930s and 1940s, Robeson made a series of statements seemingly calculated to outrage ordinary Americans, black as well as white. After a 1934 visit to the Soviet Union, where he was welcomed as an honoured guest and his son attended school with Stalin's daughter, Robeson claimed that he felt freer there than in the United States. He continued singing in this key through World War II, when his public appearances were typically made on behalf of Russian War Relief.

Robeson's greatest notoriety came after the war, when America had to face the threat of Soviet aggression in Europe and Asia. Reiterating his claim that in Russia he had "walked the earth for the first time with complete dignity," he added such fanciful assertions as that Peoria, Illinois, had been taken over by fascists, and that "fascist Greece" and Franco's Spain were more of a threat than Russia to the American people.

Then he dropped the real bomb. On April 20, 1949, speaking before the "World Peace Congress" in Paris, he declared that American blacks would not fight for the American flag, least of all against Moscow. "It is unthinkable," he insisted, that his race "would go to war on behalf of those who oppressed us for generations." Russia, he said, was "a country which in one generation has raised our people to the full dignity of mankind."

There weren't many more "African Russians" then than there are now, but the uproar that followed Robeson's Paris declaration had nothing to do with the status of Slavic blacks and everything to do with the attitudes of ordinary black Americans.

Walter White, leader of the National Association for the Advancement of Coloured People, told the press: "We do not feel that Mr. Robeson voiced the opinion of the overwhelming majority of the 14 million Negro Americans. Negroes are Americans. We contend for full and equal rights and we accept full and equal responsibilities."

The next year, White went further: "Paul Robeson is wrong in giving consent by silence to a political way of life whose strategy is amoral and subject to reversal whenever it suits the whims or fears of a tiny group of men in the Kremlin... Russia's eloquent and perfervid denunciations of colonialism and race prejudice have been singularly meaningless to me ever since she sold oil to Italy to crush Ethiopia [in 1935]."

Protests against Robeson were not limited to the American blacks whose patriotism he had impugned. The day after his Paris statement, an audience in Stockholm whistled and booed when it realized he was singing the Soviet national anthem, the first verse in Russian and the second in English. A melee erupted and many of the concertgoers stormed out. Robeson then told a hastily-called press conference that democracy did not exist in the U.S., and that "only in the Soviet Union can we Negroes walk in the streets just as everybody else can." In other words, even Ethiopia was more racist than Mother Russia.

Robeson later cancelled concerts in Copenhagen because they were sponsored by a daily newspaper supporting the North Atlantic Treaty, which created N.A.T.O. At another press conference, he said he considered American democracy the same as "Hitler fascism." In Oslo in 1949, he followed the example of other intellectuals captured by the Stalinists – men like the gifted American novelist Henry Roth, who at the party's behest silenced himself for thirty years – when he declared that henceforth he would perform only for political ends: "I have no time in the political struggle of today to entertain people. I am sorry." The statement, with its false humility, was supremely arrogant, as if the destiny of humanity depended on him and his option for Stalinism.

Thus, Paul Robeson voluntarily gave up the career which it is claimed he lost to "McCarthyism." Worshippers at the shrine of anti-anticommunism apparently believe that personal losses caused by immoral political decisions should be compensated for by public apology if not financial reparations. Yet nobody would make such a claim on behalf of the American poet Ezra Pound, whose allegiance to the Axis during World War II led to years of confinement in an insane asylum as an alternative to a treason trial. Pound's propaganda for Hitler and Mussolini nearly sent him to the gallows, even though he mainly delivered it toward the end of the war, when the Axis represented no direct threat to his country. By contrast, Robeson made his remarks when America's security was by no means assured.

It is not widely known today that the Kremlin's strategy toward American blacks was a central element in Stalin's plan to turn the cold war into a hot one. Democracy had fallen in Prague in 1948, Berlin was blockaded, and Stalin was prepared to invade dissenting Yugoslavia. More importantly, Robeson publicly encouraged American blacks to refuse service in the U.S. military just as North Korea's Kim Il Song received a final Soviet go-ahead to launch the Korean war.

Robeson received the Stalin Prize the year the dictator died, and signed a eulogy expressing a grief in which Robeson found himself completely bereft of his vaunted eloquence. "Slava – slava – Stalin, Glory to Stalin," he babbled. "Forever will his name be honoured and beloved in all lands."

The suggestion that Robeson betrayed his country would provoke howls of rage today. American, many British, and some other European intellectuals observe a double standard: Fascist enemies of democracy, such as Pound, the philosopher Martin Heidegger, or the critic Paul de Man, were criminals; but Communists were democracy's best friends.

On return to the U.S., in June 1949, Robeson again insisted that it was "unthinkable that the Negro people of America or anywhere else in the world could be drawn into a war with the Soviet Union. I repeat it with a hundredfold emphasis. They will not." On the same occasion he declared: "I love the Soviet people more than any other nation... It's up to the rest of America when I shall love it with the same intensity that I love the Negro people from whom I spring... In the same way that I deeply and intensely love the Soviet people."

Paul Robeson made his choice; and the "rest of America" made its decision, consigning him (until recently) to a merciful obscurity. The man has no more business on a U.S. postage stamp than the Revolutionary War traitor Benedict Arnold or the assassin of Abraham Lincoln, John Wilkes Booth.

–The American Spectator, July 1998

Thinking About Conlon Nancarrow

The news of the death of Conlon Nancarrow comes a week after that of William S. Burroughs, making the former seem a luminous double to a dark star.

Apart from Conlon Nancarrow it would seem difficult to imagine someone who better represented the concept of "Yankee ingenuity," once considered a virtue. In fact, Nancarrow appears as a kind of ideal American of the 20th century: talented, passionate, curious, brave, idealistic, creative. And he was a true "internationalist," as he showed in his service in the International Brigades in the Spanish Republican Army, as well as his long residence in Mexico.

I grew up in a milieu dominated by classical and experimental music; my father was a concert performer and collaborated with Harry Partch, Nancarrow's peer.(1) But I knew nothing of Nancarrow until the beginning of the 1970s when I encountered the circle of the music publisher Peter Garland, who edited the review *Soundings*, and who would later publish Nancarrow's scores.

At that time I was absolutely committed to literature, and especially to the study and translation of André Breton, and I was impressed by the discovery that the catalogue of Garland's publications included a reprinting of one of Breton's least known and clearest texts, *Silence d'Or*, as translated by Louise Varèse, wife of the composer Edgar Varèse. In it, Breton dealt with music: music composed and performed, that is to say, something other than the verbal music to which Breton was so well suited. At that time, and even today, it has been assumed that Breton was, so to speak, an enemy of formal music, and that Garland would republish such an essay showed a certain daring on his own part.

Nancarrow was a topic of continuous discussion in Garland's circle, along with the newly influential tradition of the gamelan, brought from the island of Bali and promoted by the California composer Lou Harrison.

My attention was also attracted to the boldness, or one might better say, the revolutionary attitude, with which Nancarrow dealt with "problems of interpretation" through his works for the player piano. He was a worthy successor to John Cage – who was perhaps the sole truly great avant garde artist produced by the United States – in experimenting with the limits of "musical technology." The youngest musicians and sound engineers encounter in Nancarrow, as in the work of Cage, a permanent inspiration.

---

(1)For a discussion of Harry Partch, John Cage, Lou Harrison, and other experimental musicians mentioned here, the reader is directed to the author's *From West to East: California and the Making of the American Mind*, New York, The Free Press, 1998.

We must turn back to the past and study the details of his political life, for one must not forget, one must never forget, that Nancarrow exposed his body to gunfire in defence of a social ideal by enlisting as a volunteer in the Spanish civil war. Had the aim of one of Franco's soldiers been surer, responding in a way no less automatic than Nancarrow's player pianos, we would never have enjoyed his compositions.

At the 20th century's crossroads of modernity, over which Lenin and Freud, Einstein and Duchamp presided, we find an unavoidable rotation in which dark totems alternate with brilliant heroes. Conlon Nancarrow is among the latter, a rare example of absolute creative integrity.

–Reforma [Mexico City], August 17, 1997
Translated from Spanish by the Author

Revisiting Scoundrel Time

By now, we've all heard the tragic story: how anticommunist witch-hunters descended on Hollywood in 1947, imposing a blacklist and driving talented men and women of conscience out of the industry. The victims were merely innocent liberals in a hurry, and the effects on American cinema were devastating.

The story is a perennial favorite. Lillian Hellman, in the decade before her death in 1984, made a virtual second career out of mainstreaming her version of "Scoundrel Time." More recently, on October 27, 1997, exactly 50 years after the U.S. House of Representatives' Committee on Un-American Activities heard the hostile testimony of the witnesses known as the "Hollywood 10," the Motion Picture Academy of Arts and Sciences – once, let it be noted, execrated as an anti-trade union body by Hollywood lefties – hosted a commemorative evening in Hollywood. The audience reacted with stormy applause as prominent actors like Billy Crystal and Kevin Spacey re-enacted the roles of the "10" as heroes in a never-ending struggle for freedom of speech. The theme was replayed soon after on TV in a CNN documentary, *Blacklist: Hollywood on Trial*.

But now Kenneth Lloyd Billingsley, in *Hollywood Party*, has demolished this mythical edifice. In this almost deadpan book, he shows that the "10" and their friends, far from being harmless do-gooders, were hard-core Stalinists. He details their defence of the Soviet purges, the Hitler-Stalin pact and Stalin's postwar aggression.

As the author demonstrates, these true believers sought to fill their movies with Soviet propaganda, exemplified by the 1943 Warner Brothers release *Mission to Moscow*, which extolled the purges and slandered Stalin's victims. There were many other, if less notorious, attempts to inflect Hollywood's products with Moscow's message.

If this were not enough, the party persecuted its own. Budd Schulberg was driven out of the movement's Hollywood branch for refusing to accept party-recommended changes in his novel *What Makes Sammy Run?* Later, the screenwriter Albert Maltz was subjected to his own Soviet-style inquisition for the ideological "crime" of praising the novelist James T. Farrell, an admirer of Trotsky. The actress Frances Farmer, according to Mr. Billingsley, was hounded into a madhouse after she returned disenchanted from a trip to the Soviet Union, "a land," she said, "crawling and half dead."

Some of this material has been covered by other authors, including the actor Robert Vaughn, who in his 1972 volume *Only Victims* attempted to present both sides of the story. Yet Mr. Vaughn's book gained him only obloquy from the Hollywood left. As Mr. Billingsley emphasizes, '60s radicals enthroned the "10" and the other Stalinists as "progressive" martyrs.

But Mr. Billingsley has broken new ground – especially about the Hollywood labour movement. Although the communists once dominated the Screen Writers' Guild, they never succeeded in taking over the mainstream cinema unions (despite immense efforts). Thus, while Hollywood remains one of the most unionised industries in the country, its labour movement has come to be symbolized by officers of the Screen Actors' Guild like Ronald Reagan and Charlton Heston. Both were supported by the majority of union members for their conscientious labour leadership.

In his most valuable pages, Mr. Billingsley tells the story of Roy Brewer, a labour leader in the mould of Britain's Ernest Bevin – tough in defence of his union, the International Alliance of Theatrical Stage Employees, but a stern enemy of the Stalinists. Mr. Billingsley also restores figures like the actors Robert Montgomery and Adolphe

Menjou – who both defied the Hollywood Stalinists – to their rightful place as champions of democracy.

In one fascinating anecdote, he tells how Olivia de Havilland, punished by Warner Brothers with a six-month suspension for demanding better roles, won a suit that "shook the studio system to its foundations." But Miss de Havilland, a kind of proto-feminist labour heroine, turned against the Hollywood communists after she was told to read a speech at a "progressive" event that was written by Dalton Trumbo, one of the "10."

There are also some dismaying revelations. For example, the playwright Bertolt Brecht played his committee appearance with feigned naïveté. When he was asked about meetings with Grigory Kheifitz, the West Coast boss of the NKVD (predecessor of the KGB), he answered evasively and fled the U.S. the next day. We now know from the Venona decryptions of clandestine Soviet communications that Brecht was very likely a significant informant for Kheifitz.

Even after all the evidence of recent years, only a handful of scholars and journalists are prepared to acknowledge the Stalinists in America as the totalitarian mercenaries they were. The truth about the Hollywood communists may never penetrate the film community, but Mr. Billingsley has done a great deal to set the record straight for the rest of us.

–The Wall Street Journal, December 16, 1998

The Rehabilitation of Elia Kazan

On March 21, 1999, a long-standing and bitter injustice was to be rectified. That evening the Motion Picture Academy of Arts and Sciences was scheduled to award a special Oscar to the 89-year old director Elia Kazan. The award was a direct rebuke to the American Film Institute and other movieland institutions that snubbed Kazan repeatedly since the 1970s, although he was once among their brightest lights. What amounted to Kazan's rehabilitation after decades of blackballing and smears marked a notable breach in the Iron Curtain that has long surrounded Hollywood's collective memory.

No figure in American popular culture during the 20th century was more deserving of honour for a lifetime of achievement than Kazan. The son of immigrants from the Ottoman Empire, he was successful as an actor, stage director, and novelist; and in the movies, he created masterpieces like *A Streetcar Named Desire* (1951), *Viva Zapata!* (1952), and *On the Waterfront* (1954). Yet Kazan saw his reputation savaged in a witch hunt – not the infamous hunt for Communists in Hollywood, but the later and far more destructive unofficial inquisition loosed against anti-Communists.

To understand Kazan's emblematic fate is an exercise in cultural archaeology. It requires sifting through the ruins of the intellectual Left for clues to the bizarre anxieties attached to the figure of the anti-Communist "informer." For that is the term, drawn from the lingo of the gangster, that leftists and "liberals" attached to Elia Kazan. More than any other personal journey, his life shows how, in the aftermath of America's confrontation with Stalinism, history demonstrated its capacity for producing contradictory outcomes and claiming human sacrifices.

Elia Kazanjoglous was born in 1909 to a Greek family in what was then Constantinople. Four years later, his father moved the family to New York and opened what became a prosperous carpet business. The young Kazan graduated from Williams College and studied drama at Yale. Along the way, he picked up the nickname "Gadget" or "Gadg."

In 1932, with the political and economic storms of the Great Depression raging, Gadg Kazan joined the Group Theatre, in New York. The encounter would influence a generation of American performers. Those were days when, even with the New Deal soon in full swing, fear was widespread and real that the United States would succumb to a red revolution. The Group Theatre had been founded by the playwright Clifford Odets and other young leftists, along with such non-political figures as Lee Strasberg. In line with the excitements of the time, most left-wing theatre consisted of "agitation and propaganda" skits on the sidewalks of New York, in furtherance of Communist demands.

All that changed one night in 1935, when Odets' new play *Waiting for Lefty* opened. Unlike other left-wing dramatists, Odets was a born playwright, and his talent was fortified by his collaboration with Strasberg and Kazan. *Waiting for Lefty* was Art; not the greatest achievement in the history of the stage, but Art nonetheless.

On the stage sat a group of men, the leaders of a taxi drivers' union. The action developed around the progress of a meeting called to consider a strike. In front of the stage, between it and the audience, actors conjured up the past, the inner lives, and the secret strivings of the drivers. All present waited for "Lefty," the charismatic rank-and-file leader without whom the strike could not begin.

At the play's unexpected conclusion, the young Elia Kazan, planted in the audience, burst to the front of the theatre and shouted that Lefty's body had been found at the taxi barn with a bullet in his head. Other actors seated among the spectators leapt to their feet, shouting as one, "Strike! Strike! Strike!" In a crescendo of protest, filled with sympathetic fury at the death of the proletarian hero, the audience was swept into the chorus.

It was unforgettable. It was a revolution. The American theatre had been changed forever.

Outside the theatre, revolution failed to materialize in America, and Clifford Odets never fully realized his abilities. But in the late 1930s, performances of *Waiting for Lefty* were packed, and many young people who saw it started reading the Communist weekly *New Masses*, and some of them eventually joined the Communist ranks.

The ultimate failure of Odets' career was part and parcel of the withered hopes of the radical intellectuals of his time. Notwithstanding the stirring slogans of solidarity purveyed in performance and leaflet and song, as the grim decade wore on, Soviet communism perverted and betrayed the enthusiasm of its adherents. The young Elia Kazan, who had joined the Communist Party in 1935, left it disillusioned within about a year and a half.

The horrors of Stalin's forced collectivisation and the ensuing famines were covered up (by, among others, Walter Duranty of *The New York Times*). But in 1936, the Great Purges of old Bolsheviks began in Moscow, very publicly, with the trial of Grigory Zinoviev and Lev Kamenev. As a preliminary to their execution (in the company of fourteen other victims) they were forced to abase themselves with false confessions of counter-revolutionary activity.

The Spanish civil war broke out the same year, and the international Left ardently embraced the cause of the Spanish Republic. But Soviet intervention on the side of the Republic led to the murder of revolutionaries guilty of the fatal error of opposing Stalin. It led, too, to the Left's defeat. As veteran Spanish radical Joaquim Maurín put it, once Spaniards came to see the war as a struggle between Stalin and General Francisco Franco, the brutal incipient dictator, the Republic was doomed, for Franco at least was a Spaniard. The Republic collapsed in 1939.

Within six months, Stalin hatched an alliance with Hitler, and the two mass murderers began carving up Poland. These undeniable atrocities – the purges, the betrayal of Spain, and the Hitler-Stalin pact – soured most of the young people who had been so stirred by Odets' play.

Elia Kazan, meanwhile, had become a journeyman actor and rising director on Broadway. He soon started acting in movies and directing short films. After World War II, his movie directing career took off in earnest, with *A Tree Grows in Brooklyn* (1945), and just two years later, he won his first Oscar –best director, for *Gentlemen's Agreement*.

A film starring Gregory Peck that attacked anti-Semitism, *Gentlemen's Agreement* was a landmark of early "political correctness". It caused an uproar. Talky and dated though it seems now, it established Kazan as one of Hollywood's left-wing talents. Also in 1947, Kazan joined Lee Strasberg to found the Actors Studio, first in New York and then in Los Angeles. Actors Studio taught "Method" acting, developed by the Soviet stage director Konstantin Stanislavsky. Among the school's products were Marlon Brando and Marilyn Monroe.

In 1949, Kazan's production of Arthur Miller's *Death of a Salesman* won him plaudits as Broadway's finest director. But he and Brando were poised for much greater attainments – reached in 1951, with the film of *A Streetcar Named Desire*. Lyrical, corrosive, and heartbreaking,

Tennessee Williams' creation explored the shadow side of American romantic illusions with a profundity that Miller never rivalled. *Streetcar's* frank sexuality – especially Brando's rendition of an incoherent yet charismatic masculinity – brusquely ended the era of prim Hollywood censorship.

It was then that Kazan, at the height of his fame, was drawn into the controversy over the Reds in Hollywood.

The U.S. government's investigation of Communist influence in Hollywood had begun in 1947, at a time when politically attentive Americans were caught up in the emerging Cold War. For patriotic citizens, it was a frightening period. Stalin increasingly reminded them of Hitler. Since the end of the war, Soviet armies had stayed on in Eastern and Central Europe, keeping an eye on the puppet regimes Moscow had installed. And around the world, Communists manipulated a fraudulent "peace" movement.

This last was central to the Communists' strategy toward the United States. Back when Hitler and Stalin had been allied, from 1939 to 1941, American Communists, in tandem with Nazi agents, deployed an array of pseudo-pacifist slogans – "The Yanks are Not Coming!" "No Imperialist War!" – exploiting traditional American isolationism. After 1945, the Soviet dictatorship went beyond borrowing arguments and tactics from the Nazis and actually adopted the role and methods of the fascists in its confrontation with the democracies.

Young American "fellow travellers," hypnotized by the Communist peace offensive, seemed to know nothing of even this recent past. Kazan, by contrast, vividly recalled the Stalinist betrayals of the '30s and the phoney pacifism of the Hitler-Stalin pact. Regardless of his popularity among "liberals" and his own continuing leftist sympathies, he saw communism as the enemy of everything he valued.

In April 1952, Kazan took a public stand. The previous January, he had been subpoenaed to testify before a closed session of the House Committee on Un-American Activities in Washington, holding hearings on Communists in Hollywood. He had appeared but had declined to identify his former comrades – that is, he had refused to break the silence imposed on Communists by the party's conspiratorial discipline and on ex-Communists by the manipulation of guilt.

But in the ensuing months, Kazan changed his mind. He came to believe that the secrecy imposed by the party was inappropriate in

America and that the Communists' demand for protection had been indulged too far. No previous radicals in the United States had ever claimed the protection of law for clandestine activities; no other society in history had offered its citizens rights behind which to shield political subversion, to say nothing of the espionage and terrorism to which the Communists were dedicated. How could a conspiratorial movement merit constitutional protection when its very purpose represented a repudiation of the U.S. Constitution?

On April 10, 1952, Kazan appeared before the House committee a second time, and "named names" in open session. Interestingly enough, while he knew the entire Hollywood Communist milieu in great detail, he concentrated on the Group Theatre –the Communists he had known during the revolutionary period in the mid-'30s when he himself had been a party member.

He identified nine members of the cell to which he had belonged: Odets; the late actor J. Edward Bromberg; the actor Morris Carnovsky, who had appeared before the committee and pled the Fifth Amendment (against self-incrimination); actress Phoebe Brand, whom Kazan had helped recruit; Paula Strasberg, wife of the anti-Communist Lee; actor Tony Kraber; party functionary Ted Wellman (alias Sid Benson), who with Kraber had recruited Kazan; Lewis Leverett, co-leader of the cell, and an actor named Art Smith.

Kazan recounted how party activities in the theatre world had been directed by cultural commissar V.J. Jerome and Andrew Overgaard, a paid official of the Communist International. His prepared statement also mentioned three photographers, Paul Strand, Leo Hurwitz, and Ralph Steiner, as well as a playwright, Arnaud d'Usseau, the deceased actor Robert Caille, and four members of a Communist front group, the League of Workers' Theatres.

The Group Theatre had been saved from Stalinist control, Kazan testified, by the firm stance of three anti-Communists: Lee Strasberg, critic Harold Clurman, and acting teacher Cheryl Crawford. Kazan had quit the party in 1936 because he had "had enough of regimentation, enough of being told what to think, say and do, enough of their habitual violation of the daily practices of democracy to which I was accustomed."

A month later, Odets made a similar voluntary appearance before the House committee and named Kazan, along with five of those

Kazan had mentioned; the two had discussed their testimony before appearing. None of the names they mentioned offered any surprises; all but the trio of photographers had been prominent and unapologetic in their defence of Stalinism, although Mrs. Strasberg, like Kazan, had subsequently become an anti-Communist. And, unnoticed then or later, Kazan and Odets had focused their testimony not on Hollywood but on the New York theatre scene, where no federal investigation took place and no "blacklist," real or alleged, existed.

Elia Kazan had decided where his loyalties lay, and he would never draw back. Interestingly, he suffered no immediate rejection by the Hollywood Left. In the broader scheme of things, the party and its supporters were clearly at a disadvantage. Stalin still ruled in Moscow, and war was raging in Korea, with Soviet pilots in action against U.S. and Allied forces. There was no popular Stalinist constituency in America.

In 1954, Kazan cast Brando in *On the Waterfront*, which took a bouquet of Oscars including best director. From the beginning, Kazan made clear that the film – about a trade unionist who defies peer pressure and chooses to testify against gangsters – was inspired by his own decision to speak out. "A story about man's duty to society" was the description he offered the press. The screenplay was written by another ex- and anti-Communist, Budd Schulberg. In some respects, the story paralleled and completed the message presented in *Waiting for Lefty* almost twenty years before.

Yet even after the defiant *On the Waterfront*, Kazan was spared the full force of leftist hatred. He continued to produce great work – *East of Eden* (1955) with James Dean, another of his discoveries; *A Face in the Crowd* (1957), about the rise of a radio entertainer to political power; and *Baby Doll* (1956) and *Splendour in the Grass* (1961), two more demonstrations of his skill at handling complex, intimate subjects. With *America, America* (1963), he began a series of projects overtly concerned with his own life, including his marvellous memoirs (not published until 1988). He also continued to direct for the stage and wrote successful novels like *The Arrangement* (1969).

It was only during the 1970s, in the aftermath of the political convulsions of the 60s, that a revived leftist fundamentalism more virulent than even that of the 30s emerged and found a target in Elia Kazan.

Two decades after the House Committee on Un-American Activities probe of Hollywood, a new witch hunt developed in America. It was led by "liberal" intellectuals holding that "stool pigeons" were worse than Stalinists. Why this logic did not prompt them to vilify those Americans who had denounced supporters of the Nazis – or, for that matter, "informers" who testified in murder trials – was never explained. From this point on, Kazan was dogged by a drumbeat of insults and carping gossip.

The worst damage to his reputation was done in the late 1970s by Victor Navasky, publisher of *The Nation* magazine. In full moral absolutist cry, convinced that the Vietnam tragedy had forever justified Communist claims, Navasky set out to write a kind of dual biography of Elia Kazan (bad) and Arthur Miller (good, because he had kept silent before the House committee.) But Kazan's refusal to apologize for his actions or to assist Navasky with his project stirred Navasky's rage. The result was a book called *Naming Names* that appeared in 1980.

Until that time, Kazan's creative work had carried more weight in most quarters than the Left's contempt for him. But the young aspiring screenwriters who read Navasky in the early '80s often had no grasp of Kazan's extraordinary achievements. Their only concern was to punish him for straying from a rigid defence of the global Left. The handful of former Communists he had named to the House committee – most of them outside the film industry when he testified – were transformed in his critics' minds into hundreds of victims hounded out of the business.

From then on, the contrasting trajectories of Kazan's reputation and those of the Stalinists he opposed say a great deal about the meaning of conscience in Hollywood. While Kazan was shunned, denied work, and otherwise humiliated, the "Hollywood 10" – the cell of hardcore Stalinists who sought to turn the 1947 House committee hearings into something approximating a congressional riot, and who paid for it with prison sentences – were lionized. Not only were their reputations restored, but institutions like the Hollywood talent guilds fawned over the "10" and repudiated their own supposed complicity with the establishment. While the "10" (who became nine when the courageous Edward Dmytryk broke with the group) were acclaimed by "liberals" for what amounted to Soviet patriotism, Kazan's achievements were routinely dismissed in such venues as the American Film Institute, where his American patriotism was an embarrassment.

The thick varnish of sentimentality coating Hollywood's romance with Stalinism long remained intact, impervious even to extensive revelations about clandestine Soviet activities in the United States from the Russian and American archives. We now know from the Venona decryptions released by the U.S. National Security Agency, for example, that Mikhail Kalatozov, a Soviet director and cinema functionary prominent in Hollywood during World War II, was a high ranking N.K.V.D. agent. When Kalatozov's name was brought up in the House committee hearings, the Stalinists jeered, claiming that this Soviet operative had only come to the legendary city to buy prints of movies to show back in the motherland.

But we see from the Venona traffic that Kalatozov – who would later direct the famous 1957 Soviet war drama *The Cranes Are Flying* – was a spy reporting directly to Grigory Kheifitz and Grigory Kasparov, the two N.K.V.D. station chiefs in San Francisco during World War II. (*The Cranes Are Flying* was shown to great fanfare in the Eisenhower White House.) Indeed, Venona evidence establishes beyond doubt that Hollywood was a major target of N.K.V.D. operations in the United States, fully justifying the congressional inquiry.

The latest landmark in Hollywood's ostracism of Kazan came in 1996, when the Los Angeles Film Critics Association dropped his name from consideration for its career achievement award. Instead of Kazan, the honour was presented to Roger Corman, producer of, among other films, *Attack of the Crab Monsters*.

Reviewing this dismal history, one marvels that the Motion Picture Academy broke down at last and decided on the special Oscar given in March 1999. Reportedly, actor Karl Malden, a star of *On the Waterfront*, argued the case for Kazan before the academy's board, to no dissent whatever. Industry sources pointed out that the crusade to exalt the "Hollywood 10" had been mainly an enthusiasm of screenwriters, who tend to be leftists, while directors, producers, and actors always valued Kazan's art. Indeed, among the younger generation in these fields, there is a surprising adulation of directors like Kazan, Samuel Fuller, and Robert Aldrich, despite their forthright anti-Communism. Outside Hollywood, too, it may be a sign of the times that Victor Navasky himself, while intransigent in his rejection of the

Venona disclosures incriminating the Rosenbergs and Alger Hiss, told *The New York Times* that Kazan's age, the passage of time, and the excellence of his work have softened Navasky's views. "It's a human thing," he said. "He's not physically well, and he made this great cinematic contribution."

By contrast, Abraham Polonsky, a Hollywood obscurity who would never have been heard of had he not received a House committee subpoena long ago, met a reporter with a snarl, "Has [Kazan] ever said, 'Gee, I'm sorry, I shouldn't have done that, I was wrong'?"

Well, no. Kazan refused, through the 1990s, to elaborate on these matters beyond the dignified statement in his memoirs: "I did what I did because it was the more tolerable of two alternatives that were, either way, painful, even disastrous, and either way wrong for me. That's what a difficult decision means: either way you go, you lose." No explanation whatever, of course, came from Polonsky and others so long devoted to Joseph Stalin. Did Polonsky, who died within a year of the Kazan award, ever say he regretted enthusiastically supporting the Soviet dictatorship that created Joe McCarthy?

In the late '40s and early '50s, many people, when called upon to choose between the House Committee on Un-American Activities and Stalin, chose the committee. Today, belatedly, others may be starting to see the wisdom of that judgment. It may even be that the thaw begun in the Soviet Union when Khrushchev was premier is finally reaching the sunny precincts of Hollywood.

(It should be noted that when the special Oscar was presented to Kazan, a small group of recusant leftists in the audience, led by the bovine actor Nick Nolte, demonstrated their disapproval by refusing to stand for an ovation.)

–The Weekly Standard, February 8, 1999

Dmytryk's Honourable Mutiny

Edward Dmytryk had it right. "When I die," he said, "I know the obits will read, 'one of Hollywood's Unfriendly Ten,' not director of *The Caine Mutiny, The Young Lions, Raintree County,* and other films." When Dmytryk died July 1, 1999, at 90, *The New York Times* quoted this remark without apparent irony. But the New York paper was kinder than its Southern California counterpart. Ever the house organ of the reigning orthodoxies in Filmland, the *Los Angeles Times* put a knife in the dead man's back. Dmytryk was not just a member of the "Hollywood 10" but the only one among them to publicly break with Stalinism. The L.A. paper led with a comment by Joan Scott, widow of Adrian Scott, a faithful leftist among the "10" and once Edward Dmytryk's creative partner. Her husband, Mrs. Scott said, had "contempt for informers. I hope [Dmytryk] had a bad life."

One might have thought Eddie Dmytryk wouldn't have cared about such things, because Eddie – whom I had the honour of knowing at the end of his life – was a fighter. He made movies about tests of will between men – the kind of pictures liberals were supposed to love, exposing the abuses of power that can occur even in worthy institutions. Had the Communist Party been what it claimed to be – a movement to rescue humanity from injustice – Eddie Dmytryk might have been loyal to it to the end.

Eddie, too, hated informers. The difference between him and Scott was that Eddie hated most of all the agents of the Soviet secret police who informed to Moscow on anti-Communist liberals. These agents included members of the "Hollywood 10", as well as, very likely, Bertolt Brecht and other luminaries of Hollywood's "Little Kremlin." This is now public knowledge, thanks to the Venona intercepts of secret N.K.V.D. communications published by the National Security Agency. But Eddie knew it back then – knew he himself had been used by Stalin's spies – and did something about it.

For most readers today, the "Hollywood 10" is a phrase without much context, so it's worth rehearsing the history. In 1947 the House Committee on Un-American Activities – spurred by really shocking evidence of Soviet spying in the film industry supplied by the Federal Bureau of Investigation – subpoenaed 19 prominent cinema Stalinists to testify in Washington. All 19 were activists. The first 10, Dmytryk included, made such a free-for-all of the hearing that they landed in jail for contempt of Congress.

Dmytryk, who stood up for the party even though he was no longer a member, pulled six months in a federal prison camp at Mill Point, West Virginia. During his confinement, his thinking changed, and by the end of four months, the knowledge that he had sacrificed himself for Stalin was intolerable to him. "I wanted out of my real imprisonment," he later wrote, "my association with the "Hollywood 10" and my publicly perceived ties with the Communist Party."

So he went back to the House committee and described the Stalinist conspiracy as he knew it. He refused to join those who, in refusing to testify, demonstrated their belief that, as he put it, "one must allow a seditious Party to destroy one's country rather than expose the men and women who *are* the Party. In other words, naming names is a greater crime than subversion." He went on, "That's what I call the 'Mafia Syndrome,' and I find no shame or indignity in rejecting it."

Because Dmytryk saw the Communists for the gangsters they were, a generation before this was politically acceptable, he suffered. He was an object of psychological assault for years, everywhere from academic seminars to Tinseltown nightclubs. Those who remained faithful to the cult of Joseph Vissarionovich, meanwhile, continued to style themselves martyrs for the freedom of the mind.

It hurt him. Who wouldn't it hurt? But he had made great pictures, like *Where Love Has Gone* (1964), with Bette Davis and Susan Hayward. Even as a Hollywood lefty, he made better movies than the rest of the "10," including *Murder, My Sweet* (1944), the noir classic written by Raymond Chandler, and *Crossfire* (1947), doubtless the best of all the self-consciously "progressive" films of that era. *Crossfire*, which dealt with the murder of a Jew by a racist soldier, included great performances by Robert Ryan, Robert Young, and Robert Mitchum, in addition to assorted dabs of propaganda. Adrian Scott worked with him on it. Eddie was proud of it to his last breath.

I got to know Eddie in 1996 when I asked him to read the manuscript of my book, *From West to East: California and the Making of the American Mind*. I had known two others of the "Hollywood 10", Alvah Bessie and Lester Cole, and found them extraordinarily unappealing. Neither regretted a day in Stalin's service. Dmytryk was the opposite: a real mentor.

He was also brutally honest. "You know, Steve," he told me, "I want to like your book, but it's rough going for me. I care about movies. I don't much care about all these Beatnik poets and their weird behaviour."

From the maker of *The Caine Mutiny*, it was a comment to be prized.

–The Weekly Standard, July 19, 1999

A Different Kind of Filial Piety

I suppose it is worth mentioning, right from the start, that I was a red diaper baby, like the three dozen or so contributors to *Red Diapers: Growing Up in the Communist Left.* My mother was a member of the Communist Party, my father a fellow traveller. Reading this volume, a collection of memoirs, I was reminded of the atmosphere in such a home: the subterfuge, the orthodoxy, the devotion to a foreign totalitarian power. The difference is that I have come to believe that the red-diaper experience was fairly appalling, whereas most of the contributors to this volume still think it was swell.

In any case, it was historically important. It is striking, even now, to be reminded that some prominent radicals of the 1960s came from orthodox communist backgrounds, as did at least one liberal media star. In a slightly comical selection reprinted here from his 1989 book *Loyalties,* Watergate hero Carl Bernstein reveals that when he was a boy, his parents, as "atheistic Jewish Communists," opposed his fervent desire to have a bar mitzvah. (In the end, they relented.)

But of course the radical legacy went well beyond religious questions. Thus Bettina Aptheker, the daughter of Herbert Aptheker, the ideological inspector general of the American Communist Party, became a leading student agitator when she went to the University of California at Berkeley in the 1960s. She writes here, proudly: "Of the Jewish daughter it has been written, 'To inherit a father's dream makes you the eldest son. To further his ambitions makes you heir to the throne.' " Robert Meeropol, son of Julius and Ethel Rosenberg, now devotes his life to "progressive activism." As for his parents' spying, it was simply a myth "used to sell the Cold War to the American public."

It is not hard to see why red diaper babies would grow up feeling alienated from the society they lived in: nearly everything in their childhoods was strange. Ilana Girard Singer describes (approvingly) a whole counter-universe to that inhabited by other kids. Her clothes were purchased at rummage sales to benefit the communist newspaper. *Flash Gordon* at the local moviehouse was off-limits because it was "propaganda," as were newsreels about the Korean War. Instead, "my father gave me books about real people [like] *Sacco and Vanzetti* by Howard Fast."

Ms. Singer hated her public school and much preferred spending time at a communist training centre, where the company was mostly adult. While her grade-school peers were watching *The Thing From Another World,* this serious little girl went to the so-called California Labour School to see "our movies." She cites the 1954 feature *Salt of the Earth,* an overwrought strike drama, as her favorite.

In the world of American Stalinist child-rearing, truth was the biggest problem; not so much the facts about capitalism and communism – although, God knows, these were sacrificed to ideological imperatives – as truth in a more personal sense. Thus, denials and silences were a regular part of home life: parents often hiding their activities from their children; children being asked to adulate Soviet communism while disclaiming their parents' affiliation with the party. McCarthyism was one reason for these public evasions, but it was often used as a pretext: The party had ordered members to conceal their affiliation even at the height of the ultraradical Depression years (i.e., well before McCarthy).

Although it is not acknowledged as such, *Red Diapers* is an expanded version of a set of unapologetic persecution stories published in 1985 in a privately circulated edition. At least this time around a few critical remarks are included.

Jeff Lawson, son of film industry hatchet-man John Howard Lawson, one of the "Hollywood 10", writes: "My emotional growth was stunted by the narrowness, bigotry, and short-sightedness of many of the people I grew up around." He's referring to the commies, not the McCarthyites. Ann Kimmage, daughter of international revolutionary agitator Abraham Chapman, describes her family's underground odyssey from New York to Mexico to Czechoslovakia and finally to China. They returned to the U.S. in 1963, when "Soviet, Czech, and American Communist parties could reconstruct our previous identities with the proper papers." She became disillusioned with leftist politics and condemns her "parents' all-consuming faith in an untried future and their blind intoxication with goals that turned out to be based on imagined certainties."

Still, too much is missing from this book, leaving it with the flavour of a wistful defence of what was, in the end, an atrocity. In American communist families, children were brainwashed, lured away from their natural, native loyalties to serve one of history's cruellest tyrannies. Such abuse cannot be easily pardoned.

–The Wall Street Journal, February 10, 1999

When Politics Was Everything:
Ella Wolfe, 1896-2000

On Saturday, January 8, 2000, Ella Goldberg Wolfe died in Palo Alto, California. She was 103. Given her age and infirmities, the news was not a shock. Yet her passing is much more than obituary fodder. To scholars of 20th century Communism, and to a few ex-Communists, her death is a landmark, for Ella Wolfe was the last prominent survivor of the generation that made Bolshevism a global, rather than a Russian phenomenon. With her, the line of living witness ended.

She was born a Jew near Kherson in Ukraine, and was brought to New York City as an immigrant. At 14, she met her great love, a Socialist activist named Bertram Wolfe. Four years later came the First World War, which dramatized the social ills the radical Left had decried in a way no speech or poem could. Then when Ella was 21, from Moscow there came news of the Lenin-Trotsky coup.

The way forward seemed clear. Bert Wolfe had become a leading member of the Left Wing faction of the U.S. Socialist Party, which in 1919 helped found the American Communist organization. He and Ella – by then his wife – were no mere activists handing out leaflets on street corners. They became world travellers, penetrating the sacred precincts of the Kremlin as leading functionaries of the new Communist International, or Comintern, then heading down to Mexico, where many believed the peasant revolution of Pancho Villa and Emiliano Zapata would take a Bolshevik direction. Bert Wolfe, by now a veteran of the American Communist underground, became a secret commander of the slender cadre of Mexican Communists.

But neither were the Wolfes ideological bureaucrats. In Mexico City, between meetings of Comintern cells, they became intimates of the artistic circle headed by Diego Rivera – of whom Bertram Wolfe remains the best biographer – and adorned by his nymphet lover, Frida Kahlo. The Rivera and Wolfe salons intersected with that of the photographer Edward Weston and his paramour, Italian-American actress and photographer Tina Modotti, from San Francisco. Indeed, it all had a rather Californian flavour, easy-going and life-loving, at the beginning.

But the days of Communist bohemianism were numbered. As the 1920s drew to an end, ugly realities intruded. After Lenin's death in 1924, the Comintern became a theatre for strident quarrels among his heirs, notably Leon Trotsky, Joseph Stalin, and Nikolai Bukharin. The so-called Right Wing of American Communism, headed by Wolfe and Jay Lovestone, another Jewish radical from New York, temporarily triumphed in the American party.

Lovestone and Wolfe embraced a theory that has struck numerous historians as supremely common-sensical. Known as American Exceptionalism, it held that a prosperous United States where factory workers owned their own homes and cars could not be won for Communism by the grim, conspiratorial methods employed in tsarist Russia or eastern Europe. Thus American Communism had to work out its own program and methods.

Stalin and his minions, however, understood something that Lovestone and Wolfe did not. The Stalinist Comintern had no interest in organizing the mass of American workers. Rather, it sought pliable agents to serve as spies and terrorists, and such individuals were plentiful in all the rich countries of the world.

They were misfits, alienated pseudo-intellectuals, and semi-criminal nihilists, for whom arguments over ideals and doctrine were abstract exercises not tethered to practical reality. With such recruits available, the Comintern's Muscovite bosses tired of quibbling with Lovestone and Wolfe, and booted them out of official Communist ranks, although not before the two Americans had let Stalin know what they thought of him. They were lucky to make it back to Manhattan alive.

For most of the 1930s, while a new generation of ignorant and ambitious young people flocked to the Comintern, the Wolfes and Lovestone wandered in a kind of limbo. They constituted a small sect – the Communist Party (Opposition) of America – that made some noise in its time, involving itself in a few major union struggles, then disappeared. Stalin's open betrayal of the Republic during the Spanish civil war of 1936-39 and the Bukharin purge trial in 1938 were moments of truth. By the onset of World War II Bert and Ella Wolfe had reluctantly begun to leave Communism behind.

They turned to a mainly private life, although Bert continued writing and produced his classic *Three Who Made a Revolution* in 1948. Eventually, they were invited to the Hoover Institution at Stanford, where they again became stars.

Bert Wolfe died in 1977. I came to know Ella at Hoover in 1982, at the time of my own regrettably late break with Communism. I was mainly researching the Spanish civil war, and she was a fount of inspiration. She remembered everything and everybody and was unfailingly generous. She became a friend, mentor, and confidante.

Bert did not live to see the election of Ronald Reagan and the collapse of Soviet Communism, but Ella did. Also during the 1980s, she began a third career, as the outstanding English-speaking authority on Frida Kahlo. The Mexican painter had become a global icon of feminism, and Ella was the main source for much of the "scholarship" that accompanied her cult.

Ella found the feminist canonization of Kahlo more than a little exasperating, especially as museum gift shops came to be cluttered with Frida Kahlo diaries, cocktail napkins, coffee mugs, baseball caps, T-shirts, and so on. Once, when I stupidly asked her to meet a young friend of mine interested in the subject, she replied, "Not you, too?"

I and some others who do not miss Communism at all will miss Ella Wolfe enormously.

–Reforma, January 22/The Weekly Standard, January 31, 2000

* * * * *

Chapter V:

IGNOBLE PRIZES

Pablo Neruda
[Nobel Prize for Literature, 1971]

Bill Clinton and Al Gore are big fans of the film *Il Postino*. Both men bought copies of the book from which the screenplay was adapted, according to newspaper columnist Liz Smith, and Clinton even went so far as to buy, as a birthday present for Hillary, a copy of *Love: Ten Poems* by Pablo Neruda, amatory odes by the Chilean poet who inspired the film.

Nominated for an Oscar as best movie of the year, *Il Postino* is the fictitious tale of a mail carrier who is befriended by the communist poet Neruda, who has been forced into exile in Italy because of threats by a right-wing government at home. Cyrano-like, Neruda helps the subliterate postman express his passion for a woman he loves. Neruda also lends his ideas, and after Neruda has returned to Chile, the mailman participates in a communist rally and is killed.

Il Postino was widely praised as a charming, humorous film. But at a time when we are concerned about the issue of filmmakers' debt to history and their responsibility to the truth, the real-life backdrop of *The Postman* should be of interest to the president, vice president and members of the Motion Picture Academy.

Much of the later renown of Neruda (born Neftalí Reyes) in the non-Latino world came not from his poetry but from the reputation he acquired as a Chilean diplomat defending the embattled Republican forces in their struggle against Franco during the Spanish civil war. But Neruda was anything but a freedom fighter.

In 1939, after the fall of the Republic, hundreds of thousands of Spaniards fled the Franco regime, many crossing into France over the Pyrenees Mountains. The Spanish Republican government in exile had amassed considerable money for the transport of these refugees to America. But the decision about who would be fortunate enough to gain safe passage fell to a group of Soviet agents and sympathizers, including Neruda. And historians estimate that close to 90 per cent of applications from non-communist defenders of the Spanish Republic were rejected.

On the ship *Winnipeg,* chartered by the Chilean government to rescue the exiles, Neruda played the role of a reverse Schindler. Using his official status as diplomat, Neruda made sure that passports to board the *Winnipeg* went to refugees who shared his politics and beliefs, which were those of Joseph Stalin. The rejected refugees were then condemned to internment or death in France, which soon fell into the hands of Hitler's rapidly advancing armies.

In his distinguished work *Beyond Death and Exile,* Louis Stein writes, "The [Spanish] anarchists claim that the transport organizers always gave priority to Communist applicants... In practice, [anti-Communists] were given a disproportionately small share of the available places." A leading anti-Communist leftist, Federico Solano Palacio, went further, declaring that some 86 per cent of the applications for transportation by anarchists were rejected. Palacio specifically cited the example of the *Winnipeg.*

As a historian of the Spanish civil war, I read with shock the "political testament" of the Catalan labour historian Josep Peirats, published in 1993: "Before World War II stopped all departures, [three ships] sailed to Veracruz, Mexico. Later on, the *Winnipeg* sailed to Chile... These trips were administered by the Communists... They granted or denied passports [and] strictly screened passengers at points of embarkation. The same procedure applied to transport to Chile, where Pablo Neruda, the Chilean poet... did the screening."

Neruda's services to Stalin did not end with this sorry episode. In May 1940, the Mexican communist muralist David Alfaro Siqueiros, in a preview of a successful assassination three months later, led a mass armed attack on the Mexican residence of Leon Trotsky, in which an American guard was kidnapped and murdered. Siqueiros, facing nine separate criminal charges, was released on bail. But soon after, Neruda helped arrange for him to get a Chilean passport. Siqueiros immediately fled Mexico, thus squelching a major part of the Trotsky murder investigation. For the rest of his life, Neruda expressed his undiluted pride in this action.

He also never bothered to hide his great enthusiasm for Stalin. Upon Stalin's death in 1953, he wrote a heartfelt threnody declaring:

To be men! That is the Stalinist law!
... We must learn from Stalin
his sincere intensity
his concrete clarity
... Stalin is the noon,
the maturity of man and the peoples.
Stalinists, Let us bear this title with pride.
... Stalinist workers, clerks, women
take care of this day!
The light has not vanished.
The fire has not disappeared,
There is only the growth of
Light, bread, fire and hope
In Stalin's invincible time!
...In recent years the dove,
Peace, the wandering persecuted rose,
Found herself on his shoulders
And Stalin, the giant,
Carried her at the heights of his forehead.
... A wave beats against the stones of the shore.
But Malenkov will continue his work.

This poem remains in print in Neruda's Spanish-language collected works. It has been excised from anthologies of his work in English, for obvious reasons.

In 1971, Neruda finally got the Nobel Prize he complains about being denied in *Il Postino*, much to the disgust of certain members of the selection committee, who could not forget his actions in behalf of totalitarianism. But Neruda's legacy is a dark one. This is true historically and in *Il Postino*. For the Clintons and other fans of the film, it may seem that Neruda had taught the simple Italian mailman nothing more or less than how to speak of love. But the vocabulary he left behind when he returned to Chile had to do as much with communist politics as with matters of the heart. And this language led directly to the unfortunate postman's death. In this subtext, at least, *Il Postino* captures a profound truth.

–Los Angeles Times, March 10, 1996

Claude Simon

[Nobel Prize for Literature, 1985]

Valentine Cunningham, in introducing *Spanish Front*, an anthology of writings on the 1936-39 Spanish civil war, was the first to acquaint English readers and scholars with the bizarre campaign by Claude Simon, the 1985 Nobel laureate in literature and practitioner of the French *roman nouveau* or "new novel," against the reputation of George Orwell.

Like Orwell, Simon fought in Spain, but unlike Orwell, Simon served in the ranks of the Stalinists. He made his impressions of the Spanish conflict the basis of several of his novels, including *Le Palace*. His use of these "memories" is peculiarly post-modernist, for his works are without storytelling or plot: they are assemblages of detail, seemingly with no logic aside from that of a telephone directory or a railroad timetable.

Simon attacked Orwell in a defamatory interview, alleging that *Homage to Catalonia* was "faked," without further explanation. This is a curious assertion, in that *Homage* is known, and has been defended and vindicated, for its meticulous truthfulness. Notwithstanding the bumptious comments of some foreigners, Simon included, *Homage* is recognized by the great majority of Spanish intellectuals as the best book written about the civil war in any language, including their own.

Simon further complained that in Orwell's account the street fighting that occurred in Barcelona, beginning on May 3, 1937, is "incomprehensible." Such a claim from the mouth of a French writer is surprising, given that no less a classic than Stendhal, who Simon professed to admire, showed the essential incomprehensibility of military actions, while they are taking place, to those who participate in them. The same may be said of Leo Tolstoy, perhaps the greatest novelist on war who ever lived. It is certainly true that Orwell's account of revolutionary Barcelona lacks the sectarian self-consciousness present in most leftist works on Spain written at that time. Indeed, Orwell's main concerns in the book included that of reconstructing his own state of mind and his slow coming to awareness about the nature of Stalinism and its role in the Spanish war.

Above all, however, Orwell told an accurate and truthful tale, largely uncomplicated by matters of doctrinal theory of the kind that led others to confuse the Communist attack on the Spanish Revolution, which is what it was, with "capitulation to the bourgeoisie." Orwell saw unequivocally that the Communists aimed at power alone, and he further perceived a truth that escaped many if not most commentators that came after him, even a half century later: that the old morality of the labour and socialist movements had given way to a new and sinister one.

But Claude Simon did not merely attack Orwell to interviewers. He also "borrowed" the English author and his narrative as the theme of his novel *Les Gèorgiques,* whose very title, given that the book has absolutely nothing in common with the *Georgics* of Vergil, betrays Simon's destructive obsession. Therein, he incorporates Orwell and his trajectory in Aragon and Barcelona into his own fiction.

Why should a French "new novelist" attack Orwell? One explanation might have to do with the very concept of the "new novel," and of post-modern discourse in general, as an expression of ultimate relativism. There is a possible chain of logic here: the Stalinists charged that the anarchists and syndicalists of Barcelona, along with the anti-Stalinist Communists of the Partit Obrer d'Unificació Marxista (P.O.U.M.) in whose ranks Orwell fought, were counter-revolutionaries deserving physical liquidation. In presenting the Communist combat with their enemies without supporting this claim, indeed, while specifically refuting it, Orwell recounted the events he witnessed in terms of his objective understanding of why they happened. By contrast, Simon, in "new novel" style, describes revolutionary Barcelona as an arbitrary and undifferentiated sample of reality.

In Orwell, events are confusing, but history is palpable; in Simon, history, above all the great historical tragedy of Stalinism, is absent. Orwell may have been reluctant to impose a rigid system of classification on the phenomena he observed, but he drew compelling conclusions. For Simon there are no lessons, and there is no fundamental truth, to be gained from examining the Spanish war and the experience of Orwell. This is post-modernism epitomized.

It is difficult not to conclude that this flight from the truth, from authenticity, is deliberate. Simon does not simply ignore the truth; he wishes to make us forget it. And for that reason his choice of Orwell as a target is appropriate, for in every atom of his being, especially in Spain, Orwell was committed to recording the truth, and to making it undeniable and unforgettable. It is perhaps ironical that, while the French "new novelists" became famous for their immersion in the petty details of physical existence, Orwell derived his sense of the direction of events in the Spanish revolution and counter-revolution from daily life.

At the point in *Homage* where Orwell begins to express his unease with the decline of the revolutionary impulse in Barcelona, he presents evidence overwhelmingly drawn from personal knowledge: the reappearance of fashionable women's clothing and the availability of gourmet meals to those with money. It was a situation where, to paraphrase Orwell, fat men feasted on roast quails while children begged for bread in the streets. But throughout Orwell's Spanish narrative, one shares his awareness that the propaganda of the leftist parties and reportage of the foreign press were far less reliable as a source of information than the witness of one's own eyes and ears, given common sense and, therefore, the ability to understand one's daily observation. Orwell reaffirms the wisdom of the Greek pro-Socratic philosopher Herakleitos, who commented, "Eyes and ears are poor witnesses for those who have brutal souls," a phrase applicable to the entire sorry spectacle of the pro-Soviet intellectuals.

Claude Simon, for his part, was proud to be counted among the permanent enthusiasts of Soviet Communism, and perhaps that alone explains his attempt at undermining Orwell. In his Nobel lecture, on December 9, 1985, he inexplicably referred to *The New York Times* as "only one of the two giants whose monstrous weight today is crushing us," because the newspaper's reporters had not found any American literary critics who knew who he was. (It is unfortunate that no reporters asked him to identify the second such colossus.)

Further on, he ascribed the general global ignorance of his work to an anti-Communist conspiracy, declaring (in 1985!) that "the Soviet Union remains, in certain circles, the symbol of redoubtable social forces hostile to social stability, forces with which I, a simple writer, flatter myself I am associated." He found "no small recompense" in that his writings were, according to him, "ranked among the instruments of revolutionary and subversive action." He even quoted Marx's *Das Kapital* in defence of his "work," or rather "labour," a juvenile conceit.

But in his Nobel lecture Simon also alluded to something that might best explain his assault on Orwell, who risked death at the hands of the Soviet secret police, as well as the Franco forces, in Spain. Simon proclaimed his affinity with the experimental genius of impressionist painting, and declared his defiance of the "conservative powers" who "held in a state of backwardness" the "great public" – thus explaining the embarrassing fact that nobody had read his books. And he complained that a French mass circulation weekly had blamed the entire affair on the Swedish Academy "having been infiltrated by the Soviet K.G.B."

A strange allusion, that. Or, considering the strange career of the literary Nobels, an indication of knowledge beyond what one might expect.

–Expanded from Spanish Marxism vs. Soviet Communism:
A History of the P.O.U.M., 1988

Rigoberta Menchu
[Nobel Peace Prize, 1992]

The award of the Nobel Peace Prize to Guatemalan revolutionary advocate Rigoberta Menchu is a multiple score for "political correctness", serving not only the obvious aims of Columbus-bashers and unemployed Sandinista groupies, but also those of certain highly-placed European meddlers in Latin American affairs.

Menchu has been presented to the world as a human-rights activist, and the Norwegians have chosen to honour her as a symbol of "peace and reconciliation." In reality, she is a major figure in a campaign to impose on the elected, civilian government of Guatemala a political arrangement with the Communist guerrillas of the Guatemalan National Revolutionary Unity (U.R.N.G.). Rather than representing peace and reconciliation, Menchu stands for continued guerrilla struggle.

In effect, the Nobel committee has put itself on the side of the declining revolutionary left in Central America. Excited at the possibility of forcing a leftist outcome on the political development of a small and faraway country, the Norwegians wish to keep the momentum going by granting their token indigenous American the most powerful form of moral support available to them. Indeed, in March 1992,

Oslo was the site for the first contacts between the legal government of Guatemala and the guerrillas, according to the Mexican news agency Notimex.

Menchu, to emphasize, does not support peace; she supports left-ist violence. She does not even accept non-violence as a means of protest. Some media noted, delicately, in the aftermath of her award, that she denies being an actual guerrilla, "but is uncritical of the rebels." As the *New York Times* put it, Menchu has "endorsed insur-rection... but says she never belonged to any of the country's guerril-la groups."

In reality, although Menchu herself is unwilling openly to declare herself a Marxist, the narrative she dictated to ghost-writer Elisabeth Burgos-Debray, *I, Rigoberta Menchu* – which has become an element of the politically correct canon on campuses around the English-speaking world – reveals an immense pride in her contribution to "the revolution." (Burgos-Debray, not surprisingly, is the ex-wife of Régis Debray, onetime Che Guevara groupie and hagiographer, and fashionable gadfly of the French Socialist government.)

In a manner reminiscent of Mao, Menchu divides Guatemalan women into four classes: "working class women, peasant women, poor ladino women, and bourgeois women." Is this really the outlook of a typical Guatemalan Indian? Elsewhere, she embraces revolutionary sabotage, acclaiming the action of those who destroy sugar-harvest-ing machines: "Our idea is to put into practice the methods initiated by the masses when they evolved their 'people's weapons': to be able to make Molotov cocktails."

I, Rigoberta Menchu is so transparent a work of propaganda for armed revolution it is amazing so few in the media commented on it following the award. Dinesh D'Souza, in *Illiberal Education*, argued that the vocabulary employed in *I, Rigoberta Menchu* is not her own but a projection of the feminist and ultraradical views held by the tran-scriber Burgos-Debray. Even C. Vann Woodward, like Régis Debray once a high priest of the left, scoffed at the idea that a transcription of an oral biography by an "unlettered woman" – to use Woodward's phrase – should be received as a modern classic.

Burgos-Debray – a Venezuelan anthropologist who directed the Institut Français in Seville, Spain, a haven for revisionist studies of the Columbus expedition – may be responsible for the strident intrusion of such First World feminist concerns as the repudiation of marriage, a real rarity among Central Americans, Indian or not. That *I, Rigoberta Menchu* is a propaganda product created by Burgos-Debray for Menchu to sign is, in the end, unarguable.

In an interview in Mexico in July 1992, Menchu insisted on placing all blame for the slow progress of government-U.R.N.G. peace talks on "the government's hard-line stance." She also called for U.N. intervention, supported by diplomatic pressure, to force the elected government to adopt the militarist-left U.R.N.G. as an equal partner in negotiations. This demand conforms exactly to the guerrillas' line: U.R.N.G. spokesman Hector Nuila said that "as long as it is not acknowledged that there is conflict in Guatemala, it will be impossible to find a negotiated solution to the situation in that country." The same spokesman said his organization would intensify its activities to force the government and the armed forces to negotiate.

Thus, the goal of the campaign by Menchu and her supporters is to legitimise an armed extremist minority acting against an elected, civilian government. Menchu's cause is not that of peace and reconciliation, but of murder and subversion, as the Nordic snobs responsible for this ridiculous award know full well. Perhaps promoting violence in a distant country of which they know nothing will console them for the failure of radical ideas in their own part of the world.

–The American Spectator, January 1993

* * * * *

Rigoberta Menchu, 1992 Nobel Laureate for Peace and a world-famous advocate for the rights of Central American Indians, has been exposed as a liar in her 1983 book, *I, Rigoberta Menchu.*

Since its publication, Ms. Menchu's "autobiography" has been accorded such acclaim that it appears in the literature, political science and anthropology curricula of many U.S. universities. Ms. Menchu's story has also inspired at least four children's books, in which she is presented as a role model.

The hoax was laid bare by David Stoll, an anthropologist and expert on Mayan Indian culture. In a new book, *Rigoberta Menchu and the Story of All Poor Guatemalans,* Mr. Stoll shows that while Ms. Menchu described herself as a child agricultural labourer who couldn't speak or write Spanish until adulthood, she actually attended two private Catholic boarding schools. Whereas she claimed her family had been dispossessed from its land by white oppressors, the property was actually lost in a quarrel with her father's Indian in-laws. A younger brother who died of starvation was imaginary, as was the burning alive of another brother at the hands of the Guatemalan military.

Mr. Stoll's book has received wide attention, including front-page coverage in the *New York Times*. Yet the fakery involved in Ms. Menchu's book is, for some, old news. In *Illiberal Education*, published in 1991, Dinesh D'Souza argued that the vocabulary of the volume was not that of Ms. Menchu herself, but rather represented the feminist and ultra-leftist fantasies of her ghost-writer, Elisabeth Burgos-Debray. Ms. Debray is the ex-wife of Régis Debray, groupie of Che Guevara and one of France's most notorious left-wing intellectual tourists.

Still, it took most of the world seven years to learn the truth, and even with the imposture out in the open (Ms. Menchu herself has not disputed Mr. Stoll's allegations, except to tag her critics as "racist"), some of her advocates are anxious to give her a break. Her promoters view her tale as a morality play about the genocide of indigenous peoples at the hands of white invaders. They take the position that the "higher truths" they believe in are ultimately more important than the facts. In an editorial, the *New York Times* explained that Ms. Menchu's lies were ultimately of small account next to the "criminal oppression of indigenous peoples in Guatemala." Geir Lundestad of the Norwegian Nobel committee also dismissed the story, stating that "all autobiographies embellish to a greater or lesser extent."

Yet the hypocrisy of Ms. Menchu's liberal apologists goes far beyond a willingness to overlook her mendacity. They also overlook the substance of her politics. Ms. Menchu was a functioning leader of the U.R.N.G., the Marxist guerrilla movement that wreaked havoc on Guatemala for decades. Insisting on a policy of unconditional victory, she declined to enter peace negotiations, even after she had received her peace prize (which she celebrated as a house guest of former Sandinista secret-police boss Tomás Borge).

To be sure, Ms. Menchu's is not the only recent case of the counterfeiting of memoirs. A similar controversy recently erupted about an alleged memoir of the Holocaust, *Fragments,* by "Binjamin

Wilkomirski." Like Ms. Menchu, Mr. "Wilkomirski" reputedly fabricated details of his life, turning himself from the illegitimate child of a Swiss Protestant woman into a Jewish native of Latvia, and claiming to have witnessed various atrocities.

But such other cases lack the most troubling feature of Ms. Menchu's misadventure: the deliberate use of lies to advance the agenda of the militant left. The worst aspect of such deception is that it obscures the real history of societies like Guatemala. The transformation of a squalid dispute between family members over a parcel of land into a drama of indigenous victims and evil invaders involves much more than the benign recycling of apocrypha into slogans. Instead, it feeds dangerous illusions and creates easy pretexts for violence.

Of course, the aspect of the Menchu controversy most relevant for Americans is the continued use of her book in schools. Exposed as chicanery, will it now be withdrawn from required reading lists? Probably not. Seated comfortably as they are, on U.S. university campuses and the boards of Scandinavian academies, Ms. Menchu's acolytes aren't likely to hold themselves accountable for their complicity in her deceit.

–The Wall Street Journal, December 28, 1998,
La Tribuna [Managua], January 9, Diario las Américas [Miami], January 13,
El Panamá América [Panama], January 14, El Mundo [San Juan, Puerto
Rico], January 18, El Diario de Hoy [San Salvador], January 22, 1999

Dario Fo
[Nobel Prize for Literature, 1997]

In an incident reported in the *Washington Post,* and too good to have been invented, the famous writers at a Library of Congress luncheon confessed they knew little or nothing about this year's Nobel laureate in literature, Italian theatre performer Dario Fo. But one person recognized his name: Jane Alexander, outgoing head of the National Endowment for the Arts. "A very good choice," trilled America's art commissar. "He's one of our greatest living playwrights."

Excuse me, our? As a former actress, Ms. Alexander must know something about theatre, which probably explains why she had heard of him. But how is Mr. Fo, who has dedicated his life to the promotion of everything discredited, despicable, and socially destructive in modern culture, "our" (American) playwright?

Mr. Fo remains an anti-American extremist almost 10 years after the fall of the Berlin Wall – an unrepentant hater of capitalism, religion, and common decency. In a century marked above all by the twin human tragedies of fascism and communism, Mr. Fo insists the real enemy is the supermarket. In a world groping for a return to morality and religiosity, Mr. Fo indulges in primitive anticlericalism of a kind that was already passé a generation ago.

Leftist drama critic Robert Brustein, naturally, chimed in with encomia similar to that offered by Ms. Alexander, comparing Mr. Fo's award with "giving the prize to Charlie Chaplin. . . . Lenny Bruce also comes to mind, as does Richard Pryor." So the Nobel Prize, which has been awarded to authors of such significance as Octavio Paz, Isaac Bashevis Singer, and Saul Bellow, is now to be considered a kind of super-classy Oscar for stand-up comics?

In fact, Mr. Fo's works are not literature, if what is meant by literature is the refinement of language, perception, and reflection. His plays are unwatchable for anybody but those wanting to hear and see a recitation of the biases, myths, and clichés of the left. His monologues are so tedious and predictable that they have more in common with radio advertising jingles than with the works of Samuel Beckett and Luigi Pirandello, prior Nobel recipients in theatre to whom Mr. Fo tries to compare himself.

No normal theatre fan would go to see *We Can't Pay, We Won't Pay* – which glorifies the looting of a supermarket -- to say nothing of Mr. Fo's more pretentious antireligious works, such as *The Pope and the Witch,* in which the pope is portrayed as turning pro-abortion and pro-drug legalization after the administration of a "truth serum." *The Pope and the Witch* is so offensive that it stirred outrage even in ultra-liberal San Francisco when it was performed there in 1992. It was correctly viewed by critics as nothing more than a riot of Catholic-baiting prejudice that, if applied to, say, Judaism, would never have been performed.

Mercenary politics has already rendered the Nobel Peace Prize, which is awarded by Norway, contemptible. This year's recipient, leftist anti-mine campaigner Jody Williams, had been preceded by Yasser

Arafat as a corecipient in 1994 and by yet another apologist for ter-ror, Guatemalan Rigoberta Menchu, in 1992.

A similar mentality on the part of the Swedes next door now threat-ens to render the literary Nobel meaningless once and for all. For although it has been granted to writers as great as Messrs. Paz and Bellow, it was also given, for purely ideological reasons, to the Russian novelist Mikhail Sholokhov and to the Chilean "poet" and part-time Soviet secret-police terrorist Pablo Neruda. The problem is not, as many complain, that the Swedish Academy often recognizes obscure authors. In fact some less famous honourees -- e.g., the Czech poet Jaroslav Seifert and the Balkan-British prose writer Elias Canetti -- have been writers of genius. The problem is that political considerations often trump literary ones.

In a category by herself stands the 1993 laureate, Toni Morrison, one of the few awarded the Nobel literature prize in the middle rather than at the end of a career, simply because she is an African-American woman. Stanley Crouch commented at the time, "I hope this prize inspires her to write better books."

It is not hard to guess what motivates the Swedes in such behav-iour. They are, when it comes down to it, brooding nostalgics, irrita-ble that the rest of the world has abandoned the verities that help com-fort them in their long winters: guilt about wealth, resentment of suc-cess, and rejection of the values of a market economy.

Similar sentiments move Mr. Fo. In *Accidental Death of an Anarchist*, Mr. Fo insightfully described his own type, as well as his patrons in Stockholm: "They're just poor, sick manic depressives, hypochondri-acs, gloomy people, who disguise themselves as revolutionaries." Now this radical has donned the best disguise of all: Nobel Prize winner.

–The Wall Street Journal. October 13, 1997

José Saramago
[Nobel Prize for Literature, 1998]

Well, they did it again. A year after they awarded the Nobel Prize for Literature to Dario Fo, a repulsive anticlerical buffoon from Italy, the Swedish Academy has continued its run of leftist nostalgia, handing the honour to José Saramago, a Portuguese novelist and unrepentant member of that country's Communist Party.

As with last year's recognition of Mr. Fo, Mr. Saramago's Nobel drew protests from the Vatican, where the daily *L'Osservatore Romano* criticized the award as "ideologically oriented," and protested that Mr. Saramago "remains an inveterate Communist." While the Portuguese Bishops' Conference defended their countryman, the Vatican was not alone in its dissent. Polish poet Czeslaw Milosz, a real hero of intellectual integrity and 1980 Nobel laureate in literature, told the Portuguese daily *O Público:* "I am not a supporter of the writings of José Saramago. It is a fashionable kind of writing, filled with humour – but low humour. I do not support this work."

Believing Catholics are understandably appalled at the Portuguese author's corrosive attacks on Christianity, as exemplified by his *Gospel According to Jesus Christ*, published in the U.S. in 1994. Mr. Saramago's Christ has a sexual relationship with Mary Magdalene, in a scene reminiscent of Martin Scorsese's film *The Last Temptation of Christ*. What is up with the Swedish Academy? Are they, as representatives of an officially Protestant nation, fanatical pope baiters?

Mr. Saramago, even more than Mr. Fo, has pursued a political career that should have excited some concern among the Swedes. Mr. Fo was a fascist in his youth, then became a communist, and remains an extreme radical leftist. But his antisocial pursuits are mainly intellectual.

Mr. Saramago, on the other hand, as a militant member of the Portuguese Communist Party, brings with him a history of really sinister behaviour in the interest of a Stalinist agenda. This novelist has behind him an unapologetic involvement in a serious attempt to destroy the freedom of the press in his native country.

Few today seem to recall that in late 1975 Portugal was poised to leave NATO and become a new Soviet satellite. The situation in Lisbon at that time was so dire that it was compared with Czechoslovakia in 1948.

On November 25, 1975, the Portuguese Communist Party, under its hard-line boss, Alvaro Cunhal, attempted a coup in Lisbon, using leftist Portuguese army paratroops as its cat's-paw. The adventure failed, but the party had laid the foundation for the coup by a wide-ranging campaign against freedom of the press, a months-long effort that close-ly resembled the assaults on press freedom that accompanied Fidel Castro's rise to power in Cuba.

Mr. Saramago, who was then assistant editor of the Lisbon paper *Diário de Noticias,* played a major role in this provocative strategy. The future Nobel laureate was a strident promoter of "true socialism" against "bourgeois democracy," overseeing the *saneamento* or "purges" of so-called fascist elements from the Portuguese media.

As chaos deepened in Portugal, Mr. Saramago's colleagues began protesting that they were being forced to report according to the Communist Party line and that their articles were subjected to a cen-sorial "fine-toothed comb" by Mr. Saramago. Verbal complaints con-tinued, followed by the "Manifesto of the 24," in which a group of journalists working under Mr. Saramago denounced the internal cli-mate at his newspaper. Twenty-two of them were fired. Mr. Saramago, questioned about this incident in 1991, commented: "The newspa-per had a certain line and could not be turned into a kind of free tri-bune where everybody could say whatever they pleased." With the failure of the Communist coup, Mr. Saramago was forced to leave journalism.

He never left his communist ideology. Only hours before he received his Nobel, Mr. Saramago spoke at a seminar during the Frankfurt Book Fair, on the topic "Being a Communist Author Today." Clearly a double standard reigns in Stockholm and elsewhere. Nobody would sponsor a seminar on "Being a Fascist Author Today," least of all at the Frankfurt Book Fair.

The Swedish Academy is using the Nobels in literature for the same end to which their Norwegian colleagues have committed themselves by awarding the Peace Prize to such unregenerate left-ists as the International Campaign to Ban Landmines (1997), Timorese guerrilla supporters Ximenes Belo and Ramos Horta (1996) and Joseph Rotblat of the Pugwash Conferences (1995). The message is clear: The snobs of the Scandinavian academies, secure in their wealth and power, remain doggedly faithful to their leftist fantasies.

–The Wall Street Journal, October 14, 1998

115

Gunter Grass
[Nobel Prize for Literature, 1999]

The award of the Nobel Prize for literature to the German author Gunter Grass marks a new phase in the recent capitulation of the prize to "political correctness". Following its presentation to such paragons of leftist ideology as the Italian anticlerical playwright Dario Fo in 1997, and the unrepentant Portuguese Stalinist José Saramago in 1998, the Swedish academy must have looked long and hard for someone who would meet their criteria of corrosive anti-Americanism, popularity with middle-brow readers and prolific output.

However, they seem to have come up short, for although Grass was long known for his arrogant beating of tin and other drums against the political values of the West, he is no longer productive as an author and is no longer very well known. Normally, wider audiences tend to scratch their heads and ask "Who?" when the literary Nobel is announced, since the academy has so consistently favoured obscure radicals like Fo. Now they will probably respond with comments like, "Oh yes, he was a writer once, wasn't he?"

Gunter Grass became famous in the 1950s and 1960s with his Danzig trilogy – *The Tin Drum, Cat and Mouse,* and *Dog Years* – all of which sold well in many languages. They were not much in terms of literary greatness – superficial tales of life in Germany under the Nazis, with occasional shocking effects – but he won many prizes. He also decided that, as a German intellectual, it was necessary for him to be political as well as literary. He became an active supporter of the Social Democrats and toured Germany as a speaker for Willi Brandt and others. The experience seems to have gone to his head rather badly, for in the 1970s, he became a strident, globetrotting figure specializing in anti-Western rhetoric.

Doubtless the nadir of his career as a thinker came during the civil war in Nicaragua in the mid-1980s. This fat little man, always peering over the half-moon spectacles perched on his nose, with his weedy moustache and shabby donkey jacket, seemed an obvious caricature of the ultimate German leftist intellectual of the 1930s, the Marxist playwright Bertolt Brecht. He had only one message: the virtuous Sandinistas were victims of a quintessentially evil American imperialism.

I remember vividly the response of the great Nicaraguan poet and journalist, Pablo Antonio Cuadra, editor of the embattled Managua daily *La Prensa*, which faced repeated attempts to destroy it by the Sandinistas, to the speechifying of Grass: "Why is this man defending a system here that he would never tolerate at home?" Cuadra, who well deserved but would never receive a Nobel Prize, asked me in genuine puzzlement. By that, he meant that Grass promoted the censorship and suppression of journalism in a way that, had it been attempted on what was then West German soil, would have stirred him to outrage, if not bomb-throwing protest.

The great Mexican poet Octavio Paz, who received his Nobel Prize in 1990 in token recognition that not every Hispanic intellectual was an acolyte of Castro, asked the same question in public. The Latin authors could never figure out why rich writers from the First World carried water for sleazy leftist dictators. Perhaps people like Cuadra and Paz were lucky in never becoming inured to something to which the rest of us have had to accustom ourselves: the totalitarian vanity of the successful intellectual.

Grass should have known better. He had, after all, joined the Hitler Youth during the Nazi ascendancy – the kind of blot that, in the case of a rightist author, would have brought about his ostracism from the community of the civilized, but which, thanks to Grass's leftism, was considered a youthful error. However, he also served in the German army and was wounded, so his hatred of the West may have reflected something more than mere intellectual conviction.

His vapid outpourings about Nicaragua led, nonetheless, to an embarrassing encounter. He had been born in Danzig, which became Gdansk in Poland after the Second World War. In 1980, of course, the same town became the scene of Lech Walesa's proletarian campaign against Soviet communism, which began the process of the Soviet empire's fall.

With conflict raging in Nicaragua, Grass went there and then to Poland during the early 80s, in quick succession. On returning to Germany, he published an article in *Die Zeit* comparing the situations of the two countries. Grass then met with the editors of the Polish underground journal *Przeglad Polityczny* and, after discussions with them, formulated a proposal: a leading Polish intellectual should begin a correspondence with the Sandinista minister of culture, Ernesto Cardenal.

117

One could imagine how many leftist consciences in Europe and elsewhere would have been salved had this proposal gone in the direction Grass, as a Sandinista enthusiast, hoped. As he stated, through this initiative "both of the dogmatic temples of faith, capitalist and Communist, would be shaken."

Fortunately, the Poles did not fall into the trap. They directed a letter of criticism to Cardenal, beginning with the stern comment that "the Soviet temple is quite sturdy, thanks in part to your and your friend Grass's policies, and we have no desire to shake the American temple." (This statement, although rendered obsolete in 1989, remains correct for its time.) The Poles noted sarcastically how "Western intellectuals trumpet their support for revolutionary Nicaragua with the same hysterical euphoria as they did before for Cuba, Vietnam, Cambodia, Angola, or Ethiopia." The Polish workers knew very well that they and the Nicaraguan workers and peasants faced exactly the same, single enemy: Marxist totalitarianism.(1)

During that period Grass also went to live in India. Later he distinguished himself by attacking the unification of West and East Germany as a revival of the Nazi threat and equating a "strong, unified Germany" with Auschwitz. He memorably described East Germany, one of the last Stalinist states in Europe along with Albania, as a place offering "a slower pace of life and therefore more time to talk to people." But about what, precisely, considering that loose talk could lead to prison sentences? He also declared that the Communist East would bring a sense of higher purpose to the West Germans.

So perhaps the Latin Americans were wrong, and Grass might have welcomed the imposition of a Soviet-style dictatorship on his country. In any event, most recently, he assailed all Germans, who took in a third of a million refugees from the Balkan wars, as xenophobes for their deportation of 4,000 Turks, Algerians and Nigerians.

The whole mosaic should be, by now, depressingly familiar. The same self-styled guardians of the Western conscience who bestowed a Nobel Peace Prize on the lying Guatemalan propagandist Rigoberta Menchu would naturally warm to a German who dedicated so much of his life to condemning the spectre of Western democratic crimi-

---

(1) Further discussion of this incident and many like it is included in the author's *A Strange Silence: The Emergence of Democracy in Nicaragua*, San Francisco, ICS Press, 1992.

nality. The tale is becoming absurdly repetitive, but then the Nobel was also presented to Mikhail Sholokhov, a miserable plagiarist, and to Pablo Neruda, an accomplice in the murder of Trotsky.

Perhaps the best attitude to these matters was enunciated long ago by André Breton and his French Surrealist comrades, who declared that all literary prizes were contemptible. Certainly, literary permanence over time has little to do with prizes – every year literate folk laugh at the list of those who never won a Nobel Prize, such as James Joyce or Jorge Luis Borges, and those who did but are unread today, such as Pearl S. Buck. But it really is a bit too much to see the prize turned into a diploma for recalcitrant enemies of Western freedom. Perhaps Paz should have refused his.

–The Spectator [London], October 9, 1999

Ismail Kadare
[Perennial Nobel Aspirant]

The very existence of the Albanian novelist Ismail Kadare, given the isolation of his country from the world, has been treated as a kind of miracle. He has been praised by the American writer John Updike and championed by the *Boston Globe,* and was the subject of an "At Lunch With" profile in the *New York Times.* Since the mid-1980s a multinational lobby has urged that he be awarded the Nobel Prize for Literature. In Paris, *Le Figaro Littéraire* opines, "We have said it before and we will say it again: When is Stockholm going to recognize the extraordinary calibre of this writer?" Kirkus Reviews welcomed his latest novel to be published in English, *The Three-Arched Bridge,* by saying, "This is a masterpiece. The Nobel can't come a moment too soon."

With Albania beset by chaos and poverty, the Swedish Academy may eventually find it an irresistible temptation to award the Nobel to Albania's only famous writer. But it would be a grievous mistake to give it to Ismail Kadare, and not just on literary grounds.

The Three-Arched Bridge, written in 1976-78 and published in France in 1981, is in many ways a typical Kadare work: less a novel than a parable, superficially undemanding but rich in subtextual meaning, and set far in the Albanian past. Narrated by a 14th-century monk on the eve of the Turkish conquest of the Balkans, it rehashes a motif from local folklore: the walling up of an innocent victim inside a building under construction, as a human sacrifice to assure the structure's completion and long survival.

One day, an unknown traveller has an epileptic fit next to a raging stretch of river served by a ferry crossing. A wandering fortune teller claims the seizure is "a sign from the Almighty that a bridge should be built here, over these waters." As we soon find out, it is most likely a hoax, staged by a devious builder of roads. A bridge-builder arrives to design and erect a three-arched bridge, which is mysteriously damaged on several nights.

Soon a "collector of folktales" arrives to research a local ballad, which tells of three brothers who worked as masons, erecting a fortress in northern Albania. Each night the work they had done by day was destroyed by mysterious forces, until they decided to immure one of their wives.

After hearing several versions of this ballad, the "collector of folktales" disappears forever. Almost immediately, travelling minstrels are performing, in local inns, a version of the ballad that has been slightly altered. The new version proclaims that a human sacrifice will allow the bridge to withstand the onslaught of the river. The road-builders begin promising money to anyone who will be a willing victim. But these balladeers, too, are frauds. As becomes clear by the end of the book, it is the ferry company – and nothing supernatural – that has been sabotaging the bridge. The ballad merely provides a pretext for the road-builders to murder one of the ferrymen's saboteurs in order to establish control over the profitable river crossing.

The tale is authentic, simple, and alluring, and its pagan and brutal underpinnings seem to offer a way to understand the recent Balkan wars. What's more, it is easy to see how such a tale appeals to current politico-literary obsessions. There is a nice deconstructionist point to the way hegemonic commercial interests in the early days of capitalism hijack a people's folklore, and put it to the service of monopolistic consolidation. Kadare, then, can be seen as a capable writer lucky enough to appeal to the literary taste of the Western academy in a way he may never have intended.

But, less innocently, Kadare was also highly thought of by the political and intellectual establishment of his native land for three decades.

For almost all of that time, Albania was ruled by the brutal ultrana-tionalist dictatorship of Enver Hoxha, fabled for his last-stand Stalinist orthodoxy. During the Hoxha regime, official favour did not come without assiduous courting – or, to put it less kindly, conscious col-laboration.

Kadare's first novel, *The General of the Dead Army* (1963), was trans-lated into French in 1971 and later turned into an Italian feature film. It is the tale of an Italian army officer sent to Communist Albania to repatriate the corpses of Italian soldiers dead in World War II, and it offers a comparison – too obvious to be called subtextual – of the morbidity and decadence of fascist-capitalist Italy with the socialist vitality of Albania under Hoxha. It is merely a deft execution of the Stalinist genre of socialist realism,(2) but it charmed the leftist youth of Italy and France, thrilled to find a product of the proletarian "Tibet of Europe" that could be called a literary work of any kind.

Many of Kadare's novels followed a heavy-handed political agen-da. His *Chronicle in Stone* was an homage to Gjirokastra, the southern Albanian town that was the birthplace of Kadare, as well as of Hoxha; the compliment to the dictator was obvious to Albanians. *The Great*

---

(2) Readers of this essay may be interested to learn that it touched off a remark-able controversy, involving Kadare himself, the writer Noel Malcolm, and the author of the present book, in *The New York Review of Books*, beginning on November 6, 1997. The relevant texts may be reviewed at the NYRB's website; most of them were also published in the Kosovar Albanian weekly *Zëri*, June 3, 2000. Mr. Malcolm took great exception to my description of *The General of the Dead Army*, protesting, that it was "absurdly described" in this manner, and that it was "utterly different in spirit from the 'socialist realist' novels of the time, with their bright sunshine, cheery peasants, and hydroelectric dams." Unfortunately, with this comment, Mr. Malcolm merely exposed his ignorance of the socialist realist genre. "Tractor romances," although abounding in Communist countries, were not the only "social realist" form. Numerous "social realist" classics pro-duced in Russia, such as Nikolai Ostrovsky's *How Steel Was Tempered*, Boris Polevoi's *A Story About a Real Man*, Aleksandr Fadeyev's *The Young Guard*, or, in China, Lu Hsun's *The True Story of Ah Q*, had nothing to do with tractors or cheer-ful collectives or the builders of dams. Rather, they dealt with revolution, war, and oppression. Kadare's *General of the Dead Army* is a "social realist" classic – as Kadare himself insisted on numerous occasions – precisely because it used the images of capitalist decay and socialist vitality in a way that was not immediately obvious. Mr. Malcolm, who fancies himself an instant expert on everything, overstepped himself badly in this instance.

Winter (1978) attacked Nikita Khrushchev, but only to exalt the unreconstructed Hoxha by comparison. (Both of these novels also included repellently approving depictions of the murders of dissidents). While *The Great Winter* was one of Kadare's failures, more and more of Kadare came out in French. At one point, Hoxha, a Francophile who had been a French instructor before coming to power, shared his own translator with Kadare.

By the time Albanian communism collapsed in 1990-91, Kadare was a genuine hit in France. Almost as soon as the cracks appeared in the regime of Hoxha's anointed successor, Ramiz Alia, Kadare decamped from Albania to France, and publicly took his distance from the Communist dictatorship. Albanians offered differing explanations for this action. Some gave him the benefit of the doubt as a born-again anti-Communist; others thought Kadare merely feared reprisals when the regime collapsed, a real probability in Albania, with its traditions of blood feuds and revenge. Kadare, meanwhile, has presented himself as a long-time dissident who had walked a tightrope under communism.

It is a deceitful claim, for Kadare was in fact an approved author of the Albanian dictatorship. At the moment of his "defection," he was vice-chairman of its official political structure, the so-called Democratic Front. Kadare had originally become known in Albania as a journalist directly serving the Hoxha regime, and as a poet. His poetry is, of course, unknown to most of his foreign cheerleaders, a blessing for him, since his most famous work in verse is his cycle *What Are These Mountains Thinking?* (1962-64):

> The long mountain caravans were waiting,
> Waiting for a leader,
> Albania was waiting
> For the Communist Party.

In other poems, widely quoted in Hoxha's Albania, Kadare wrote:

> With you, the Party
> Even terrible pain
> Is finer than any joy...

And,

There will be light.
No, the Bible is not speaking,
But the Party. Its roaring voice
Resounds through people's hearts like loudspeakers...
We, the poets of socialist realism,
Are also there,
With notebooks of verse in our pockets
Turning, there where molten steel is poured.

Kadare also issued a number of extraordinary attacks on non-Communist Albanian and foreign culture. In his 1997 speech, "The Literature of Socialist Realism is Developing in Struggle Against Bourgeois and Revisionist Pressure," he declared, "In their spirit, in their content, even in their style and intonation, many of the works of the present-day decadent bourgeois literature are reminiscent of the Bible, the New Testament, Qur'an, the Talmud, and other tattered remnants of the Dark Ages."

This from a man who has since become famous ransacking medieval Albanian tradition for the raw material of his stories.

In the same discourse, Kadare attacked the "decadent modernism" exemplified by the French poet Guillaume Apollinaire. Why Apollinaire, of all people? Because Apollinaire was deeply influenced by his friend the Albanian writer and patriot Faik Konica – Apollinaire even wrote his great love poem "La Chanson du Mal-Aimé" in Konica's house in London – and Hoxha had judged Konica a "reactionary."

In 1988, Kadare penned a tribute to Hoxha, already three years dead and therefore beyond threatening him, but praising the dictator as "an outstanding intellectual, and an erudite humanist." As late as 1990, he described the Albanian-American poet Arshi Pipa, an opponent of the Hoxha regime, as "diabolical... an absolute spy... an old hyena."

Many Albanian intellectuals are dismayed that a man who served communism as Kadare did might be awarded a Nobel as "Albania's greatest writer." In 1993, the Albanian dissident author Amik Kasoruho published a survey of Kadare's work in a small Albanian language periodical issued in Italy. Kasoruho, the son of an executed anti-Communist, himself served 10 years in Hoxha's prisons. After his release he was barred from literary activity because of his "negative family background." What Kasoruho found worst about Kadare was that he opted for such conduct when it was not "absolutely necessary." Kadare chose to join the chorus of Hoxha's hacks, Kasoruho emphasized.

After years of assailing the "archaic" quality of Albanian culture, Kasoruho alleged, Kadare has come to embrace it – unsurprisingly, since it lends itself so well to the entertainment of Western readers. But Kasoruho also charged that Kadare had done something far worse than merely change his literary style. He had constructed his later fictions by looting the works of non-Communist writers whose achievements and reputations he had helped suppress. Kadare's *Doruntine*, for example, was based on a tale recorded by the outstanding folklorist Donat Kurti, who disappeared into Hoxha's prisons. *Broken April*, a novel about North Albanian blood feuds, drew on the work of Shtjefen Gjecovi, the "reactionary" Albanian scholar who died before communism came, but whose work was also attacked by the Hoxha regime and treated with contempt by Kadare.

Such habits add a weird element to the disappearance of the "collector of folktales" in *The Three-Arched Bridge*; Kadare sought to assure that real collectors of folktales vanished from cultural memory. But, of course, just as the "collector of folktales" is portrayed in that volume as the pawn of commercial interests, so were Kurti, Gjecovi, and others so labelled under the Hoxha regime, as agents of Western influence.

Kadare attacked many of the great creators of Albanian literature, even though they had recorded the materials from which he drew such writings as The *Three-Arched Bridge*. Their names, unknown abroad, include Konica, Gjecovi, Kurti, Bernardin Palaj, and Lazer Shantoja – the last two executed by the Communists. Other Albanian authors disapproved of by Hoxha, such as Gjergj Fishta (the national poet, who died in 1940 but whose bones were dug up by the Communists and thrown in a river) and the great émigré poet Martin Camaj, are beloved among Albanians, but are also unknown to the mass of foreign readers today, in large part because all interest in Albanian writing was and remains absorbed by publicity for Kadare.

Kadare has attempted to make up for these offences in various ways. In 1991, after arriving in Paris, he published a set of reflections, *Albanian Spring*, reproducing his correspondence with Hoxha's successor Ramiz Alia, along with various self-serving jottings. In it, he mentioned "attempts to make people disappear from Albanian literature," specifically mentioning Konica and Fishta, as if he himself had not been one of the main individuals responsible for such "disappearances."

Nobody should underestimate the pressures Kadare faced as a writer under the Hoxha regime, or deny him the right to reinvent himself in the aftermath of communism's fall. But to leap from understanding to wholesale absolution for his past – and even strident calls that he be crowned with the world's greatest literary honour – involves something other than the rights of an author,

Kadare's appeal comes largely from his exoticism. To call him exotic is only to say that Albania's other great writers remain a closed book to readers in the West. And if that's the case, it's at least partly because of the help that Kadare gave the Hoxha government in suppressing them.

Someone in Sweden ought to know that.

–The Weekly Standard, March 24, 1997

* * * * *

Chapter VI:

CONTEMPORARIES

Breyten Breytenbach

Breyten Breytenbach, considered the best modern poet in the Afrikaans language, first received substantial publicity in the English-speaking world in 1977. At that time, he had been imprisoned in his native South Africa for some two years. A further legal proceeding, based on charges of terrorist activity while in prison, brought him to the attention of the liberal and Left communities in Britain and the U.S. In 1982, thanks to efforts by French president François Mitterrand, Breytenbach was released. Within a few years, he published *The True Confessions of an Albino Terrorist*, a semipoetic account of his trials and imprisonment. It was widely reviewed, with Joseph Lelyveld, in *the New York Times Book Review*, typically comparing Breytenbach's martyrdom to that of the Russian poet Osip Mandelshtam, who was imprisoned and eventually consigned to an anonymous death in the Siberian labour camps for writing a poem attacking Stalin. The South African poet even made it onto the American television chat show circuit.

Let us begin with Breytenbach himself, his origins and his literary work. Breyten Breytenbach was born in 1937 in the heart of Afrikaner society. His two brothers were active supporters of the South African establishment, with one serving as a commanding officer in the South African forces in Namibia, the other affiliated with the state security agencies. Breyten became a prominent member of the group of non-conformist Afrikaans writers known as the *sestigers*, or 60s generation, a group which also includes the novelist André Brink.

The very existence of such a group clashes with the image Western liberals came to adopt of Afrikaner society and culture, but that is another story. Breytenbach's poetic style is a distinctively affecting mixture of surrealism and philosophical pessimism: his wit, and his austere figures, come across rather invitingly in English translation. He is also a talented painter, and when he left South Africa in the mid-1960s he went to live in Paris. There he met a Vietnamese artist, Yolande Ngo

Thi Hoang Lien, and married her. Yolande became the central subject of his creative work, which developed into an extended erotic meditation drawing on Buddhist and other Asian sources. Unfortunately, Yolande's Asian ethnicity also barred Breytenbach from returning to South Africa in her company: their case clearly contradicted the country's then-standing laws against racially-mixed marriages.

The conflict between Breytenbach's love for his wife and his identification both with the South African landscape and with the Afrikaans language drove him, in the years that followed, into an extreme position on the apartheid regime. By 1975 he had formed an organization at first called Atlas and then *Okhela* ("Spark" in Zulu), made up of South African whites living in European exile and collaborating with the African National Congress (ANC). Like the ANC, *Okhela* saw its future in armed struggle.

In the mid-70s Breytenbach chose to return to South Africa, utilizing a false passport in the name of Christian Galaska, a French citizen. His mission was to set up a network of Okhela supporters and black activists, included the ill-fated leader Steve Biko (who died in detention in 1978); the practical aim was support for black trade unions. As *The True Confessions* hauntingly recounts, in South Africa Breytenbach was tracked down and arrested, as he was preparing to fly back to Europe.

At this point the story becomes complicated. When he appeared in court Breytenbach presented himself as a contrite, erring son of the Afrikaner nation, pleading for forgiveness. Even more curiously, the Left, in South Africa and elsewhere, which had done little enough to help him after his arrest, altogether backed off from any further association, denouncing him as a renegade and stool pigeon. He was sentenced to nine years' imprisonment, and had served two (entirely in solitary confinement) when the charge of terrorism from within prison walls returned him to court in 1977.

During the second trial, while the pro-ANC Left continued to hold him at arm's length, an informal network of artists in Europe and North American began working to organize and express some form of solidarity with him. It was then that I became involved. I had been active in a related matter concerning Argentina, and through a literary acquaintance in Holland was asked to participate in the Breytenbach effort. I did so, becoming the head of the Committee on

127

the Breytenbach Case, based in San Francisco but circulating materials through the United States. I received a continuous flow of documentation on the affair from Europe. We published bulletins describing the poet's progress through the second trial, which ended in a minor fine; we then concentrated on demands for his release.

In May 1978 a new item was introduced into the mosaic. I received from my European contact a clipping from a South African newspaper, reporting the assassination in Paris of Henri Curiel, an Egyptian Jew who had been a close associate of Breytenbach during the latter's European exile. Curiel had been identified in the French press as a "mastermind of terrorism," and was described by the South Africans as "the mystery man who sent Breytenbach to South Africa clandestinely." An accompanying note from my European correspondent stated that Curiel had indeed maintained an "underground organization for training [in] guerrilla warfare, counterfeiting passports, instructing in coded information methods." Furthermore, that the passport given by Curiel to Breytenbach before the latter's flight to South Africa "probably was in fact a trap," and that Breytenbach had been "set up by some Stalinists (or, say, Moscow-oriented... activists), who... subsequently tipped off... the South African secret police."

It would be hard for someone not in my situation at that moment to imagine the impact this letter had on me. My European friend was unchallengeable as a source of information. The very possibility that a man of Breytenbach's talent as a writer and painter could have been so offhandedly sacrificed by Soviet agents called to mind the queasiest moments of Stalin's own reign. Too, the idea was not reassuring that our little group of pro-Breytenbach activists might have been simply victims of our own enthusiasm. We had committed resources and time, attracting a certain degree of harassment from defenders of South Africa while also working in a kind of moral quarantine, regarded with ill-concealed hostility by the rest of the anti-apartheid movement in the United States. We had thought the coolness of our pro-ANC contacts was a product of racial suspicion that could be overcome considering the human rights aspects of the case and its potential for embarrassing the Pretoria regime. We were wrong. The Breytenbach affair was much more of a potential scandal for the South African Left than for the country's then-rulers.

For the plain truth, as Breytenbach's book confirmed at numerous points, was that he was betrayed. "I was betrayed even before I arrived [in South Africa]," he declared flatly. "It was not my idea to go down there but I had to submit myself to the majority decision... Stupidly vain, when told there were certain things which only I could do, it touched me, and I fell for it." And who, then, was responsible for this? "My dear, ineffective, fat, institutionalised friends in the liberation movement... those professional diplomats, those living off the fat of the suffering of our people back home and who've done so for years and will do so until they die." And why did this sleazy drama transpire? Because Breytenbach had begun to question the Stalinist tendencies dominating the South African Left. "To my shame as a South African I have to admit" that the Communist Party of South Africa "was among the first organizations lauding the Soviet Union for its invasion of Hungary and again later of Czechoslovakia." As for Curiel, that he "was a KGB operative had crossed" Breytenbach's mind. "It's really not so far fetched... some of his oldest friends quit... because, they say, he was using [them] as a vehicle to serve the Soviets... He never made any bones about his total commitment to orthodox Soviet communism, call it Stalinism."

The full betrayal involved in the Breytenbach case is only comprehensible through a further digression on the Curiel case, a strange matter in its own right. Although I dropped out of touch with the Breytenbach enthusiasts in Europe soon after receiving the clipping and letter on Curiel's assassination – I was simply too shocked and demoralized to continue – I remained interested in learning more about Curiel. In 1981, Claire Sterling devoted a full chapter of her book *The Terror Network* to Curiel, in which she claimed that the process ending in the latter's assassination in Paris had begun when Breytenbach, disillusioned and abandoned in prison, divulged information on the Curiel network to the South African secret police. She noted that, presumably on the basis of Breytenbach's information, Curiel's terrorist support network had been exposed in the French weekly *Le Point* in 1976. In a highly interesting titbit, she also pointed out that Curiel was the cousin of the famous British subordinate of Kim Philby, George (Bihar) Blake, who has been described as the most effective of all Soviet spies.

Late in 1984 Jean-François Revel became involved in the Curiel controversy when, in *Encounter*, he defended *Le Point*, for which he writes, against a pro-Communist French author, Gilles Perrault, who had produced a massive apologia for Curiel titled *A Man Apart*. Perrault's opus, an incredibly prolix exercise in revolutionary "hagiography," to use Revel's term, depicted Curiel as a hero of Third World solidarity and peace, more concerned with arranging meetings between Israelis and moderate Palestinians than with his admittedly "fanatical" admiration for the Soviet Union. Perrault failed to address the charges in Claire Sterling's book, which appeared three years before his, or to deal with the association between Curiel and Blake. He did, however, state that those who sent Breytenbach to South Africa knew he was headed for disaster.

During the Breytenbach solidarity campaign of 1977, we tried to portray him as a victim of a kind of treason on the part of his Afrikaner parents and brothers. But as his memoirs prove, his Afrikaner family stood by him with greater loyalty than was shown by his adopted "family of the revolution." This brings us to the real tragedy of Breyten Breytenbach. It is not that a talented artist was temporarily locked up by a repressive regime against which he had plotted violent resistance, but rather that such an individual should accept his betrayal, as he seemed to do in his memoirs, and place the blame on his own "weaknesses" as an intellectual. Breytenbach has as yet done nothing to subject his leftist mentors and betrayers to the kind of searching moral inquiry one took for granted must be addressed to his Afrikaner compatriots, including his own relatives. (This statement remains true 15 years after it was first put in print.) In this he resembles no one so much as the character Rubashov in Arthur Koestler's great novel about Stalinist betrayal, *Darkness at Noon*.

By now it should be obvious to all that the world is a curious and cruel place, in which the sentiments of a poet and painter are easily perverted by such paradoxes as the need to find a new family relationship where one's own has been unsatisfying. Breytenbach seemed to have learned from this experience: he declared that from then on he would concentrate on his poetry and painting. Yet this, I believe, was the wrong lesson. Breytenbach was no Mandelshtam, and the comparison is specious: Mandelshtam lost his life for writing a single poem, whereas Breytenbach, after participating in a revolutionary conspiracy, came out of prison safely. But neither should Breytenbach allow himself to become a Rubashov, one who accepts his degradation at the hands of his putative comrades. At least the person on whom the fictional Rubashov was based, Nikolai Bukharin, attempted to subvert the 1938 Moscow trial in which he was judged and condemned. In this respect, Breytenbach had, and still has, much to learn.

–Commentary, October 1985

David Horowitz

Late in 1987, David Horowitz and Peter Collier, both former editors of *Ramparts* magazine and ex-New Leftists, sponsored an assembly of disillusioned radicals in Washington, D.C. The gathering, titled the "Second Thoughts Conference," was seen by Horowitz as an opportunity for the outstanding anti-radical intellectuals of two previous generations to pass the torch of righteous anti-communism to Horowitz and his cohort. But after much talk – in which I, as a former leader of the revived Young Communist League in the America of the 1960s, and recent convert to free-market economics, was proud to participate – the torch was not passed.

Hilton Kramer of *The New Criterion* and other elders excoriated us "Second Thoughters" for remaining mired in 60s psychology and for refusing to admit that we had been, in the words of John Maynard Keynes, "a generation of immoralists." Irving Kristol was dismissive: "I'm already on my third thoughts." Depressed almost to tears, Horowitz paced the marble lobby of the Grand Hyatt hotel, asking, "Why wouldn't they do it? Why wouldn't they acknowledge us as their heirs?"

The answer can perhaps be found in the trajectory of Horowitz's own career. Horowitz first came to attention in 1962 when his book, *Student,* an engaging examination of the early protest movement in Berkeley, California, was published. Eager to develop a theoretical underpinning for an emerging New Left seeking to distance itself from the Stalinist apologetics and practices of the Old Left without abandoning the dream of a democratic socialism, Horowitz wrote two canonical texts of the new radicalism: *The Free World Colossus* (1965) and *Empire and Revolution* (1969). These titles were accompanied by numerous ancillary works largely devoted to a revisionist view of the origins of the Cold War. Horowitz and Collier would go on to write a series of best-selling biographical studies of powerful American families: *The Rockefellers* (1977), *The Kennedys* (1984) and *The Fords* (1988).

During this period, Horowitz grew increasingly disenchanted with the refusal of many of his former comrades to denounce the thuggery of Black Panthers who had committed crimes in the name of revolution. Moreover, he began to despise the apologetics made on behalf of revolutionary regimes in the so-called Third World and the dogged anti-Americanism that seemed to deform so much of the New Left critique. It was then that his "second thoughts" began. He began to see himself – and to be regarded by many of his former allies – as the Whittaker Chambers of the New Left. However, unlike Chambers, the former high Soviet agent in the U.S., whose autobiography *Witness*, is an essential item in the literature of communism, Horowitz, despite several attempts (see his anti-'60s polemic *Destructive Generation*, published in 1989, and his 1997 autobiography, *Radical Son*), had yet to write so formidable and indispensable a work. And Horowitz's out-of-court testimony about the crimes of the Black Panthers, although impassioned, hardly bear comparison with Chambers' denunciation of Alger Hiss, which placed a "generation on trial," in the memorable words of Alistair Cooke.

The publication of Horowitz's *The Politics of Bad Faith: The Radical Assault on America's Future* offers an opportunity, once again, to examine why he continues to fail to measure up to the standard set so many decades ago by Chambers. The new book is not, as its title and subtitle would have us believe, about "the politics of bad faith" or "the radical assault on America's future." It is not at all about America's future (or even much about its present). It is a set of essays on the failure of Marxist-Leninist ideology, an ideology in which Horowitz, a certified red diaper baby, as the children of American Communists are known, grew up.

Horowitz begins grandly, evoking in his introduction "a conflict that for two hundred years has dominated the political history of the West." This is at best a slipshod formulation. The controversies underpinning the Cold War and America's later culture wars may seem to "have their origins in the French Revolution, when radicals sat to the left in the National Assembly and their opponents to the right," as Horowitz insists. But such a scheme is badly skewed. Factional and ideological polarization is nothing new. Recall the Sadducees and

Pharisees in Judea during Roman times; as for the oft-maligned French Revolution, it produced Jacobinism and the guillotine, the inspiration for Leninist politics, as well as the most philosophically elaborate version of modern bourgeois democracy. But Horowitz rarely lets the facts of history get in the way of a good story.

The problem is that the story he tells has been told better before. The core essays in this book are "The Left After Communism" and "The Fate of the Marxist Idea." Unfortunately, nearly everything relevant about the broad failures of communism – why it failed as a political movement and why it failed as a system of governance – has already been said (and said with greater eloquence and insight), beginning 90 years ago with the anti-Bolshevik polemics of the Mensheviks and continuing through the chronicles of Alexander Solzhenitsyn, among others.

Nevertheless, Horowitz inexplicably seems to believe that the history of counterrevolutionary thought begins with him. He is disconcertingly uninterested in the struggles and sacrifices of the numerous individuals who preceded him on this well-worn path of secular apostasy. It is as if anti-communism in the 20th century consisted of little more than Chambers, Leszek Kolakowski (who is his other major intellectual hero) and, surprise, David Horowitz. The man's hubris is breathtaking. The achievements of such figures as George Orwell, Arthur Koestler, Stephen Spender and others in Britain, as well as Lionel Trilling, Clement Greenberg, Nathan Glazer, Seymour Martin Lipset and Gertrude Himmelfarb, to name but a few in the U.S., are so much greater by any measure than those of Horowitz and other 60s ex-radicals that even to suggest an ideological continuity is absurd. And that is to say nothing of such figures, generally neglected today, as Nikolai Berdyaev, André Breton, Ante Ciliga, Jean Malaquais, G.P. Maximoff, Josep Peirats, Gustav Regler, Wilhelm Reich, David Rousset, Victor Serge, Manés Sperber... the list is long indeed. There is more of value in the following passage from Joseph Roth's "Trotsky novel," *The Silent Prophet*, than in the whole of Horowitz: "We want to help. But we are not born for that. Because of our impotence, nature has endowed us with too strong a love, it exceeds our powers. We are like a man who is unable to swim, but who jumps in after a drowning man and goes under himself. But we have to jump. Sometimes we help the other, but usually both of us go under. And no one knows whether, at the last moment, one feels happiness or a kind of bitter anger."

Still, Horowitz retains admirable qualities. Rooted in his radical origins, these virtues are his large-scale outlook, his interest in history and his commitment to morality in political life. Unlike so many of his generation, Horowitz, at least, remains an activist, passionate in his conviction that ideas matter. In this regard, he offers an immense contrast to the great majority of his opponents as well as his rivals. The post-60s radicals, particularly those who found themselves in the American academy, have assumed, with rare exceptions, an appallingly uniform narrowness, rigidity, ultra-specialization and, above all, narcissism, since the social explosions of 30 years ago. Indeed, they match or exceed their conservative counterparts in their addiction to prejudice, self-righteousness and indifference to the consequences of their postures and actions. Horowitz, for all his bitterness and self-importance, continues to care more about the fate of ordinary Vietnamese, Nicaraguans and other people around the world than about the need for American intellectuals to feel good about themselves.

He is at his best in a chapter called "The Religious Roots of Radicalism." Here he takes on one of the few themes in anti-radical literature not to have been adequately developed by others. He is fascinating when he writes about the Kabbalah of Rabbi Isaac Luria and about the school of Jewish mysticism that eventually transformed the anxiety of Jews at the universal chaos of the 16th century into belief in the imminent arrival of a messiah. Horowitz advances the view that Lurianic messianism began the radical temptation of Jews in modern times. But, as elsewhere, he goes too far. Pious Jews will almost certainly be offended by Horowitz equating Lurianic Kabbalah with the serpent in the Garden of Eden. Horowitz suggests that both offered humanity a God-like existence. Religious Jews will be outraged by the comparison for, in addition to the insult to Luria, one of the most saintly figures in Jewish history, Horowitz ignores the fact that Jewish mysticism has always sought to promote "godly" or "heavenly" behaviour – behaviour that has only very rarely led to immediate messianic frenzies.

Horowitz is a curious case. He sees clearly the danger of the messianic temptation in others but is unwilling to recognize the illusion in himself. He remains, at heart, a man with a mission; only the mission has changed. Once a man of the left, he now is a man of the right. However, his *modus operandi* remains, remarkably, the same. The rigidity at the core of the ideology Horowitz now so fervently promotes, the prosecutorial zeal with which he pursues his enemies (both real and imagined), betray a man uncomfortable with a more charitable and complicated view of the world he inhabits. He refuses to abandon a morally absolutist world-view. That is a pity. His refusal cripples his critique.

Horowitz, in the end, has much in common with Chambers but, alas, falls short of his hero's example. Still, he is the closest thing we have to a Chambers. Unlike Horowitz, Chambers somehow succeeded in seeing himself objectively, avoiding a public role as a single-minded, hectoring Jeremiah. His example remains exemplary. Horowitz may yet surprise us, but on the evidence of this slim volume, it is unlikely.

–Los Angeles Times, October 11, 1998

Christopher Hitchens

Christopher Hitchens and I do not agree about very much. For example, as a friend of Albania and Albanians, I will never forgive his assault on the outstanding Albanian personality of our time, Mother Teresa. He loathes Norman Podhoretz and esteems Susan Sontag; for me it is quite the reverse. But when I heard that the U.S.-based British provocateur had blown the whistle on Sidney Blumenthal in the Clinton investigation – and was being savaged by the left for doing so – I felt a twinge of responsibility. (Blumenthal, a presidential confidante, had lied to the U.S. Senate about slandering Monica Lewinsky.)

Let me explain. I first met Hitch, as he is known far and wide, at the "Second Thoughts Conference" in Washington in 1987. He insulted me in an exceptionally rude manner, as reported in one of the American national magazines.

Then, in 1992, writing from Sarajevo for *The Nation*, he passionately and powerfully denounced the crimes of the Serb extremists. I wrote him a letter (actually, a telegram) of congratulations for his stand.

Finding ourselves, at least figuratively, on the same side of the Bosnian barricades, we put our scrap at "Second Thoughts" behind us.

Thereafter he would occasionally call me when he came to San Francisco and we would meet for dinner. At one of these occasions early in 1998, we were joined at the Washington Square Bar and Grill, the Golden Gate city's ostensible literary and journalistic hangout, by his wife and fellow journalist Carol Blue and by a female colleague of mine.

Under the dim lights and over the delectable cuisine, we argued many things. Knowing that he, like myself, had been a Trotskyist, I pointed out the most fascinating aspect of the recently disclosed Venona decryptions of Soviet secret police communications: the extent to which anti-Stalinist leftists – with whom Hitchens has always identified – were targeted by Stalin's operatives in the U.S. The top spies in Venona were much more interested in the daily affairs of the widow Trotsky, in Mexico City, even after Trotsky's death, than they were in the White House or any other logical target.

Hitchens professed doubt about these revelations. Then I sprang a question on him: "What would you think of the case of a man who desperately wanted to testify before the House Committee on Un-American Activities, but who was killed before he could?"

When I told him that the man's name was Trotsky, Hitchens was inclined to reject such bad news, almost 60 years after the fact. But over the next few months clip files and quotes from Trotsky's own writings convinced him that when the old revolutionary was murdered in 1940, he had been preparing a scorching exposure of the use of the Communist Parties worldwide by the Soviet secret police. (We now know that Laurence Duggan, a Soviet spy and head of the State Department's Division of American Republics – with responsibility for Mexico where Trotsky was exiled – lobbied actively against granting him the visa he needed to testify before the House committee.) Referring to a new book by an unapologetic apologist for Stalinism, Ellen Schrecker, Hitch reported on this twist of Trotsky's fate in the August 24, 1998 issue of *The Nation*.

In that article, Hitch discussed a bombshell in the recently published (and ineptly assembled) twenty-volume "complete works" of George Orwell. It turned out that early in the Cold War, Orwell had given British authorities a list of Stalinist apologists.

One of Hitch's *Nation* colleagues, Alexander Cockburn, who glories in the gangster-style nickname "Big Al," borrowed from a certain Capone, disparaged Orwell as a "snitch," the American underworld equivalent of a "grass." Feminine publicist Katha Pollitt wrote, "Let's say the Communist Party was bad and wrong" – purely for the sake of argument, obviously – "why should Orwell help the repressive powers of the state? Let the government do its own dirty work." How this work became "dirty" when applied against "bad and wrong" people was left unexplained; but in any event, it was presumably "dirty work" to defend Western democracy from the most dangerous enemy it ever faced. But Hitch noted that "all [Orwell's] observations mirror precisely what he was saying openly (when he could get published) about the contemporary 'fellow-travellers.'" There was nothing dishonourable or inconsistent about this. Provision of information was not the same as "informing."

People who report on their friends and associates may legitimately be called "snitches" if the charges are groundless. But those who report honestly on criminal behaviour are witnesses, not "snitches," and in Anglo-Saxon society, a millennium ago, those who knew of a crime but kept silent were held equally to blame. Calling such people "snitches" or "informers" shows the parallel between Communism and the Mafia, which similarly labels its defectors.

To "inform" on those who collected information for the K.G.B.'s terrorists was something other than schoolyard, or even gangland, "snitching." A real hero of a real revolutionary movement, the former Soviet military intelligence chief Walter Krivitsky, who defected during Stalin's purges, may have put it best. Whittaker Chambers recalled Krivitsky telling him, "In our time, informing is a duty. *Man kommt nichts leicht von Stalin los.* One does not come away from Stalin easily."

We now see from Venona that, as Trotsky declared, the entirety of the American Communist Party was involved in "snitching" on American citizens who opposed Stalin. The American Stalinists and their Muscovite masters, acutely aware of how poorly this would play in America a half-century ago, turned the tables adroitly. Those who properly denounced the "informing" routinely carried out by American Communists in the service of the K.G.B. were themselves labelled "informers."

Cockburn, who spread Stalinist-like slanders about Hitchens, is the son of a Stalinist agent, Claud Cockburn, who defamed Orwell and his comrades in Barcelona in 1937. Naturally, he, like Katha Pollitt, seized on Hitchens' defence of Orwell's "snitching" to explain his alleged "betrayal" of Blumenthal. Todd Gitlin, in the *New York Observer*, excoriated Hitch as a Trotskyite unwilling to join the totalitarian "liberals" in the Popular Front with Slick Willie. John Judis of *The New Republic* endorsed Blumenthal, defending the hatchet man of the Clintonocracy on the basis of their shared employment at *In These Times*, a leftist tabloid that tried its best, but ultimately failed to meld the politics of Tom Hayden, a Southern Californian ex-spouse of Jane Fonda and apologist for terrorism, with the journalistic methods of the *National Enquirer*, America's version of the *News of the World*. Edward Jay Epstein, who grotesquely charged Hitchens with denial of the Nazi Holocaust, first became famous serving America's enemies by attacking the Warren Commission investigating the assassination of John F. Kennedy 35 years ago.

Some things don't change after all.

–The American Spectator, April 1999

* * * * *

Chapter VII:

SOME NOTABLE FAKES

André Malraux:
The Phoney Giant

It would be hard to imagine an individual who more symbolizes the illusions, delusions, and disillusion of 20th century intellectuals than the French novelist and politician André Malraux.

Born in Paris in 1901, dead in a hospital southeast of Paris in 1976, he seemed to have seen and done it all. His outstanding novel, *La Condition Humaine* (Man's Fate), which won him the 1933 *Prix Goncourt*, also helped put the Chinese Communists on the map of the world's consciousness. Its arguments and images acted like flypaper to young minds everywhere seeking an idealistic and spiritual affirmation, the "heart of a heartless world," during the 1930s. It is the best novel in praise of Bolshevism to have been produced by a non-Soviet author, although it cannot compare with the works of Isaak Babel and Boris Pilnyak.

The decade leading to the outbreak of World War II was convulsed with crisis after crisis, as political life turned into a brutal contest between the fascist and Communist variants of totalitarian statism. Malraux became a star of a kind then rare in public life; indeed, such terms as "star" weren't yet used for such folk. But he was admired and desired by comrades and would be lovers on every continent. His personality grew to encompass all forms of passionate affirmation, from speechifying before congresses of useful idiots about the glorious advances of Soviet Communism to leading an air squadron for the leftist forces in the Spanish civil war.

With the arrival of World War II, continuing in his line of publicly advertised gallantry, Malraux rallied to General de Gaulle, and after the war he made the sensible and correct choice in favour of Gaullism, the West, democracy and capitalism against Soviet imperialist anti-Americanism. For this, he was never to be forgiven by many of those Communists and "fellow travellers" who once idolized him, although it was the best thing he ever did. And of the ex-radicals of his generation, he attained the highest responsibility in government, as a minister of culture in de Gaulle's administrations.

For the rest of his life, he spoke, wrote, and acted out in public, but without the sparkling talent he seemed to have displayed decades before. His pretentious writings about art made him the laughing stock of serious critics. This emptiness was explained by his leftist enemies as a consequence of the abandonment of his past ideals. But Malraux had never been a real Bolshevik like Whittaker Chambers or Arthur Koestler. He never wrote a Marxist pamphlet or edited a revolutionary organ, never fought in a strike, much less on a barricade, and never spied. Certainly, one can hardly imagine Chambers, by contrast, as a presidential cabinet member.

But in France, as so often, what counted was personal – even more than literary – style, and style Malraux had in abundance. Unfortunately, most of it was phoney. Although he had never served the Communist International or any other conspiratorial body as an agent, he claimed to have been a Red commissar in revolutionary China, an imposture that was taken seriously by the greatest foreign historian of the phenomenon, Harold M. Isaacs, in his magisterial *Tragedy of the Chinese Revolution.* Similarly, he posed as a hero of the Spanish Republican air force, even though he knew nothing of aviation, and never learned to fly a plane.

Yet lots of people who should known better, in addition to the normally cautious Isaacs, were taken in. Malraux gulled Trotsky, which was a real feat, although the old heretic, who had lived in Paris and met his second wife, Natalya Sedova, at the tomb of Baudelaire, was soft on French authors, having written in praise of Louis-Ferdinand Céline and collaborated with the surrealist André Breton. But Malraux was a genius, if not as a writer, then as a manipulator of image and myth. He discovered, and exploited better than anybody else, the allure of Bolshevik commissars for urban bohemians around the globe in the years after World War I. Unlike the French revolutionary thinkers who took Communism seriously, he perceived that in the West it was basically a fad.

Were his books any good? By and large, no. Even *Man's Fate,* his best, suffers from verbosity, artificiality, and excessive sentimentalism. Sartre remarked, famously, "Malraux has a style – but it is not a good one." Vladimir Nabokov, who knew better than anybody, dismissed him as a puffer and assembler of clichés.

Interestingly enough, Malraux never compensated for his novelistic services to Communism, particularly in *Man's Fate,* by attempting a serious anti-Communist work. *L'Espoir* (Man's Hope) was, along with Ernest Hemingway's *For Whom the Bell Tolls,* one of the worst books written about the Spanish civil war. But at least Hemingway noticed the moral evils present in the Soviet intervention in Spain, and was attacked by the comrades for it. Malraux, who had hinted at such issues in *Man's Fate,* seemed to decide that in Spain the cause was bigger than the ambiguities of Bolshevik conduct; by then he had his own role as an icon of the Moscow-controlled Popular Front to worry about.

But did not his choice of West over East, in 1947, reflect moral courage? Not necessarily. Indeed, just as he was absent from the ranks of writers like Chambers and Koestler in bearing literary testimony to the horrors of Communism, he was also about ten years late, when compared with them, in making a clean break.

In *André Malraux: A Biography,* Curtis Cate has done an admirable job of clearing the cobwebs of self-obfuscation from Malraux's life. Although Cate occasionally seems reluctant to criticize his subject's flaws, he suppresses nothing and excuses little.

The real Malraux was a risk taker who more resembled a sociopathic drifter or criminal than a man of letters, or even an old-school revolutionist. His adventures involved testing the duties and responsibilities of ordinary life more than the dangers of ideological or physical combat. He was, then, the classic bourgeois in reaction against his background, and, at that, a dandy playing at revolt more than a real rebel. As he himself wrote with inordinate narcissism, as if he were the first ever to conceive such a pedestrian and essentially inaccurate notion, "Almost all the writers I know like their childhood; I detest mine." His father represented, of all possible bourgeois horrors, the worst: he was a stockbroker.

The young André, seeking placement even as a youth, failed to get into the Lycée Condorcet, the most prestigious Paris upper school of that time, where the poet Stéphane Mallarmé had once taught. He then decided to dispense with further education, dropping out, as one might have said several decades later. However, the teenager had already, as a hobby, acquired a serious knowledge of the rare book and illustration business, and, predictably, this served him well. In a development that smacks more of the 19th than the 20th century, and which would seem nearly impossible today, he furthered his literary training by selling, rather than studying, books.

Soon he was himself publishing minor critical pieces, and by 1920, with the Dada excitement at its height among the writers and artists of Paris, he was working for Simon Kra, a legendary avant garde publisher. Then he met his first wife, Clara Goldschmidt, at a literary soirée; she was the educated daughter of a very rich leather merchant. For the next several years, Clara bankrolled Malraux's ventures.

His enterprises were varied, if nothing else. After much effort, he succeeded in entering the exclusive publishing circle around *La Nouvelle Revue Française*, the greatest literary monthly of the century, as a book reviewer. But his budding career seemed to wither, as he lost work and money, the latter through disastrous investments.

Cate notes that the truly great French writer, Guillaume Apollinaire, took a humble clerk's job in a bank when he found himself in similar straits, and used his paychecks to treat such friends as Picasso to dinner. But the resourceful Malraux was unprepared for such a sacrifice. He had already figured out a way to grow rich quickly and easily. There were, he told his bride, small Buddhist temples in Cambodia from which exquisite statuary could be easily removed for resale in the United States.

Thus, Malraux's first great project was a fling in vandalism and looting. The couple went to Cambodia, then a part of French-ruled Indochina, and located a temple unknown even to nearby villagers. They ripped seven carved cornerstones, two representing protective goddesses, out of the walls and boxed them up. Of course, on their way back to Saigon from the rainforest, Malraux was arrested.

This despicable incident made his reputation, for once the news of his being sentenced to three years in prison as a pillager of temples was publicized, his Paris colleagues leapt to his defence, mainly led, in a disconcertingly unthinking manner, by Breton. Breton may have recalled how his mentor Apollinaire had once been similarly (but falsely) charged, in a theft of statuettes from the Louvre, and besides, Breton was also an avid collector of non-European art.

In any event, the hue and cry out of Paris assured that Malraux would be spared any jail time. The affair could be said to have determined the course of his career, for he had learned how easily intellectuals could be manipulated, and that literary swindles were easier to pull off than direct robbery.

André Malraux was the exact opposite of the man with whom he eventually most sought to identify, T.E. Lawrence. Lawrence, although no minor faker himself, and equally the advocate of a questionable cause, namely Arab nationalism, seems to have, at least, served self-lessly, facing the greatest physical and intellectual challenges. Lawrence then modestly withdrew into a form of silence; by contrast, Malraux spent his life in a campaign of propaganda for himself. Cate's account of this long exercise in dishonesty suffers from occasional gaffes and minor errors, but it teaches us many lessons. Above all, that many 20th century intellectuals, and most of the people who admired them, were rather despicable fools.

–The American Spectator, October 1997

Ernesto "Che" Guevara:
The Glamorous, Gruesome Guerrilla

Who was Ernesto "Che" Guevara? In the aftermath of his death, 30 years ago, his image remains among the most famous in the world. It is hard to imagine that someone like Hillary Rodham Clinton or Cherie Blair did not own a poster of Che in the late 60s and early 70s. His features were then the symbol of revolution, launching a thousand insurrections.

But today his personality, as opposed to his picture, remains near-ly forgotten, known primarily in his native Argentina and among a fringe of enthusiasts in the West. His evanescence illustrates many of the less understood aspects of the 60s Left, above all the ephemeral quality of the period and its protagonists. A biography, *Che Guevara: A Revolutionary Life*, by Jon Lee Anderson, written with official support from the Castro dictatorship, in which Che played a major, early role, is clearly intended to revive interest in him.

Che, as an idol of youth, was more than a man – he seemed omnipresent, his impact permanent. Yet his entire career as a world-historical figure lasted no more than nine years, from 1959 to 1967, and his legacy, if it exists at all, is meagre. His appeal grew out of the "anti-imperialism" directed against the democracies, particularly the United States. But the main thing to say about him is that he dripped charisma and physical magnetism. When he, Castro, and others in the Cuban revolution burst onto the scene, their primary attraction was their youth, their looks, and their sense of style. They had more in common with Brando, Elvis, and Kerouac than with Marx, Lenin, and Trotsky. Their challenge to established society was neither intellectual nor abstract, but hormonal – it was, in the authentic Latin American tradition, macho.

The future revolutionary was born in 1928, conceived out of wedlock, his birth record correspondingly falsified. His parents had left Buenos Aires for the hinterland almost immediately after their marriage, to avoid gossip. As Anderson notes, ambiguities about Che's life would persist until his end: His death certificate, after his execution in Bolivia following his last, failed insurrectionary campaign, was also faked.

The Guevara family was not at all poor. Che's father worked in various enterprises, including construction contracting. Che, when he was 14 or 15, lost his virginity in a typical upper middle class way: with the servant of a friend. Though this was the era of Juan Perón and his hysterical wife Eva, the elder Guevaras were not Peronistas. They were standard Latin American leftists – anticlerical, favourable to the Republicans during the Spanish civil war, and active supporters of the Allies during World War II, when Perón and his cohort, melding traditional Argentine dislike of "British imperialism" with admiration for the fascist "new order," tilted the country toward the Axis.

By the time Che reached manhood, Brit-bashing was somewhat old hat among the Argentine young. Nonconformists like "Ernestito" gravitated toward Marxian socialism and regarded the United States as the enemy. Guevara acquired a ferocious case of Yankeephobia early on, and it never left him. While training to be a doctor, he travelled widely in South and Central America, even as far as the U.S. These trips allowed him to refine his socialist and revolutionary views, and they also led him into contacts with K.G.B. agents that marked out a path he would always pursue: alliance with Moscow against Washington.

In 1954, the 26-year old Guevara defended Guatemala's Soviet-influenced regime, fighting on the losing side. The next year he met

Castro, the leading figure in a group of Cuban revolutionary adventurists he had encountered in Guatemala. From then on, Che was instrumental in the rise of Cuban communism and its projection as a global force. He became the world's best known theoretician of "guerrilla warfare," the forms of irregular or "low intensity" combat that, in the past, had been viewed as little more than adjuncts to regular military operations. Guevara infused the term "guerrilla" with romance, providing an antidote to the isolation of radical movements in the West.

In this early period, a serious propaganda effort was organized to present Castroism as precisely what it was not: a species of radicalism independent of, and even opposed to, the Soviet Union. The main significance of Anderson's book is its admission, supported by the Castro authorities, that the Cuban revolutionary movement, Guevara included, entered the grip of Soviet intelligence long before it triumphed over the Batista dictatorship in 1959.

Nevertheless, we have been told repeatedly that Castro did not begin as a Communist but was pushed toward Moscow by an arrogant and obtuse American President, Dwight Eisenhower. Guevara and his comrades, the claim goes, were anything but Communists, but rather agrarian reformers, in the style of Mao and his associates in the 40s, or nationalists in the mould of Nasser or Sukarno, or unorthodox demi-Marxists closer to Trotsky than to Stalin. (The same idiotic lies were purveyed in defence of the Sandinista party state in Nicaragua.) Anderson's book should end these illusions once and for all. Guevara had a longstanding relationship with a top Soviet operative named Nikolai Leonov – the kind of arrangement that put him in the category of Alger Hiss and Julius Rosenberg rather than that of, for example, the Mexican revolutionary Emiliano Zapata.

Chilling, too, is Anderson's account of the Castroites' gratuitous bloodletting, which began as soon as their insurrectionary movement became serious. Had this criminality been widely known in the 60s, it might have disgusted some of the young partisans who, around the world, flocked to Cuba's defence. Castro's brother Raul was especially nasty, a sadist, as close observers of the regime have long known. Che (who had taken the Hippocratic oath as a physician) ordered killings on short notice and without reflection. He once wrote, "I am not Christ or a philanthropist... I am all the contrary of a Christ...

145

Not only am I not moderate, I shall try not ever to be." Throughout the revolution, he demanded the execution of "spies" and "informers" as if ordering dinner. After the Castroites gained total control over the island, they killed countless of their adversaries in reprisals.

Soon, Guevara grew restless. Like Castro, he was disappointed that the Cuban missile confrontation with the U.S. in 1962 had not ended in nuclear conflict. Che was bored by administrative duties in Havana and remained beholden to the allure of a continuing world upheaval based on guerrilla tactics. He commuted from one radical "front" to another, unsuccessful in fomenting conflict in Argentina, Africa, and, finally, Bolivia. There, his band of terrorists made mistake after mistake, surrounded by Indian peasants who viewed them first with indifference and then with hostility. Che's group was eventually tracked down by the Bolivian army and wiped out; Che was executed in 1967.

When Castro announced this news to the world, some who knew the depth of rivalry within the Cuban regime wondered whether Che had not been deliberately sent to his death. An East German secret police prospect, Tamara Bunke, who had lived in Argentina while being groomed for "deep cover" infiltration into the U.S., was killed in his band. She became famous as "Comrade Tania, Che's woman in Bolivia." It could be that she and others, under instruction from Havana or Moscow, betrayed him.

In any case, Che was more useful to the international Left as a martyr than he had been alive. Posters of his sensitive-appearing face and flowing hair blossomed on the walls of university dormitories and lecture halls from Paris to Pasadena. Few who worshiped him, as 1967 turned into the climactic year 1968, knew much about his real life or ideas. Few of his admirers, outside the top ranks of the Cuban and Russian state parties, knew the extent of his bloodlust and indifference to human feelings.

For some 15 years after his death, the cult of Guevara spurred thousands of young people, in Latin America and elsewhere in the Third World, as well as in Italy and other European countries, to take up arms in guerrilla adventures, usually manipulated from Moscow. But Guevara's doctrines, even, as in Bolivia, under his direct command, could not be exported from Cuba, where rural warfare was traditional. One after another, these attempted uprisings turned into massacres, with students and other naïfs sent heedlessly into battle against superior military forces.

Today, Latin America has recognized the futility of the guerrilla utopia and has moved far beyond the leftist dreams of the 60s and 70s. Masses from Mexico to Argentina now look to liberal democracy and the free market for solutions to their problems. The end of Guevarism was visible in Peru in 1997, when the hugely unpopular Tupac Amaru movement of narcoguerrillas saw its latest grab for global notoriety, the seizure of hostages at the Japanese ambassador's residence in Lima, crushed by Alberto Fujimori.

Still, Che will not be forgotten entirely. The University of Buenos Aires has announced a department of Che Guevara studies, which will analyse the future of "liberation" in Latin America. It would be better for Latin America if Che's memory were to remain a quaint regional phenomenon, like the cult of Evita. Or the tango.

–The Weekly Standard, May 12, 1997

Daniel Ortega:
Nicaragua's Thief Executive

Managua, Nicaragua

Before the 1979 revolution, La Perfecta was one of Nicaragua's leading food companies. Founded in the 1950s by Armando Llanes, a Nicaraguan-born graduate of the Virginia Polytechnic Institute, its immaculate, modern plant produced pasteurised milk, powdered milk, ice cream, and cheese; its brand dominated the market.

While its history as a successful business venture is noteworthy, La Perfecta's curse is that it's remembered more often for its political history. That history began about a decade after its founding, and involved a young man named Daniel Ortega.

According to a 1979 memoir by Humberto Ortega, Daniel's brother and Nicaragua's long-time military chief, in the mid-1960s the Sandinista guerrilla movement embarked on a series of "systematic armed blows aimed at economic objectives... The most successful were the economic seizures carried out at branches of the Banco de America and Banco de Londres, the Lacmiel Ice Cream Company, and La Perfecta dairy, among others."

147

But the La Perfecta raid, Daniel's first, was not a complete triumph. As La Perfecta's current employees are only too happy to recount to visitors, the plant workers resisted the attempted "expropriation" and beat up the guerrillas, including Daniel. The enraged workers even killed one Sandinista, Selim Shible.

It is easy to imagine the Marxist cant that must have flowed from the mouths of the Sandinista leaders and intellectuals about the "low consciousness" of La Perfecta workers. Far from aiding the revolutionary cadres in their theft, these workers defended the enterprise that was responsible for their livelihoods.

After the revolution, the Sandinistas got their revenge. The usual pretext for nationalization was that the owners had some involvement in politics, especially in the party of the defunct Somoza regime. However, the 1981 confiscation of La Perfecta lacked even that thin pretext.

For the next decade, the Llanes family lived in exile in Miami, aiding, whenever possible, the anti-Sandinista Contras. But in 1990, Nicaraguan voters overwhelmingly rejected Daniel Ortega and replaced him as president with Violeta Chamorro, whose partisans in the anti-Sandinista United Nicaraguan Opposition demanded the return of such confiscated properties. The Llanes family returned from Miami and carried out a detailed inventory of their facility while pressing their legal case for return of its assets.

According to family scion Javier Llanes, who later worked on the staff of Managua Mayor Arnoldo Alemán Lacayo – destined, in turn, to become the conservative successor to Chamorro as president – the family's inventory revealed a set of facts that eloquently summarized the economic banditry practiced by Daniel Ortega's gang:

— A top-of-the-line machine that filled cartons of milk and orange juice was sold by the Sandinistas to a Costa Rican dairy owned by the American firm Bordens.
— A powdered milk facility, opened at the plant in 1978, was traded to another Costa Rican firm for a herd of undistinguished milk cows with a stated value of $10,000.
— A fleet of refrigerated milk trucks disappeared from the plant and was reputed to have been taken to Cuba.
— The company's ice cream producing equipment, which would

cost $1 million to replace, was either stolen piece by piece or destroyed; in any event, none of the equipment remained in the plant.

As for the family's claim to the dairy, only a small part of the overall complex was returned to it by the Chamorro government. Moreover, the transfer took place with the condition that the family accept a $400,000 debt on the property.

Further evidence of economic plunder by the Sandinistas was discovered after recovery of the plant. A Sandinista politician, José León Talavera, claimed that Mr. Ortega's government had invested $2 million in La Perfecta, based on a foreign-aid package delivered to the Sandinistas by the Finnish government. However, the Llanes family documented and informed the Finns of the truth: The money had apparently disappeared, while what remained of the plant equipment was reassessed and overvalued to cover the alleged malfeasance.

The Llanes family was committed to defending its claims but, like other defenders of risky causes, felt somewhat besieged. Mr. Talavera – with whom Javier Llanes became involved in a second conflict over the family's former country house, which was "given" to Mr. Talavera by the Sandinista army – threatened the Llanes family, leading to their hiring some of Javier's former Contra comrades as house guards. This practice increased among the business class as the country's 50 per cent to 70 per cent unemployment drove more and more people into street crime.

Like most Nicaraguans, the Llanes family became disillusioned with Mrs. Chamorro's administration, and especially with her failure to remove the criminal Sandinistas from the official positions they continued to occupy in the army, from the banks and from numerous other enterprises that they "liberated" before losing power.

Still, in Javier Llanes and many other Managuans, I encountered real pride at the small gains that had been made since Daniel Ortega was removed from his post. The currency had stabilized, consumer goods were available, restaurants and other small businesses were opening, and Managua cleaned itself up.

The horizon remained clouded by political divisions, as well as by violence, but in much of its inner being the Nicaraguan nation had changed remarkably little from the night in the mid-1960s when the workers of La Perfecta dairy met the Sandinista robbers with physical resistance. In Nicaragua, Communism had clearly taken much less of a social toll than in Eastern Europe or the former Soviet Union.

The Llanes family seemed interested in only one thing – getting the best quality food products to Nicaraguan families. Some Nicaraguan workers, including many at La Perfecta, expressed loyalty to their former bosses and looked forward, as much as the entrepreneurs, to the rehabilitation of economic resources that were degraded in the Marxist utopia.

At the same time, General Humberto Ortega complained that U.S. aid for the reconstruction of Nicaragua has been dispensed "with an eyedropper." But the justice sought by such ordinary Nicaraguans as the Llanes family, their employees and customers, and by other victims of Daniel Ortega's gang of "revolutionary thieves," was also tasted one drop at a time. Ortega's victims warned their American friends that any help from Washington should be provided under a strict condition: Property rights must be respected and property claims resolved, in Nicaragua, as elsewhere in the former Communist world.

–The Wall Street Journal, October 29,
La Tribuna [Managua], November 12, 1993

* * * * *

Chapter VIII:

HEROES

The Spanish Civil War In Historical Context

I.

On December 20, 1998, a man named Irving Weissman died in Daly City, California, a suburb of San Francisco. He was 85, and suffered congestive heart failure.

Mr. Weissman was a veteran of the Spanish civil war and World War II, and a former Communist. In the week after his demise, an obituary appeared in the *San Francisco Chronicle*. It described his birth in New York to Jewish immigrant parents; his first language was Yiddish, and he learned no English until beginning elementary school. While attending City College of New York, he was recruited into the Young Communist League. He became well-known as a street corner speaker.

Because of the Great Depression he dropped out of college, and in 1933 he joined the Work Projects Administration, a New Deal programe for the unemployed. As described to a *Chronicle* reporter by his survivors, Mr. Weissman, who had previously served as a Communist organizer among the jobless, was assigned by the WPA to teach English to new immigrants. He used the official Communist organ, the *Daily Worker,* as his text; when supervisors checked the classrooms, the students would pull out more conventional reading matter.

In many ways, Mr. Weissman was a typical representative of radical New York youth in the 1930s. But in July 1936 a distant sequence of events changed his life forever. A military conspiracy broke out against the elected leftist government of the Spanish Republic. Police loyal to the regime, joined by armed defence bodies from the ranks of the large working class parties, mainly Socialists and anarchists, successfully defended Spain's four main cities: Barcelona, Madrid, Bilbao, and Valencia. Only Seville, where the labour movement was weak and dominated by the small Spanish Communist Party, fell to

151

the rightist officers, whose forces were quickly, and inaccurately, labelled "fascist."

Almost immediately, Nazi Germany and authentically-fascist Italy were revealed to be supporting the military rebels; German transport planes were used to ferry troops from then Spanish-controlled northern Morocco, where the uprising began, to the mainland near Seville. Soon, Italian "volunteers" were on their way to strengthen the antigovernment ranks, which had come under the overall command of General Francisco Franco, head of the Spanish Foreign Legion.

Ultrarevolutionary leftist groups in France, Britain, Belgium, and Scandinavia, including numerous Italian and German antifascist refugees, viewed the salvation of the Spanish cities by labour-based forces as a workers' revolution. The prominent role in defending Barcelona of the anarchosyndicalist *Confederación Nacional del Trabajo* (National Labour Confederation) or C.N.T., the largest of Spain's radical factions and the only mass revolutionary union grouping in Europe, inspired anarchists, syndicalists, and their sympathizers to head for the Pyrenees and the Spanish frontier.

Trotskyists and other anti-Stalinists, members of minuscule political sects, joined the southward stream from the beginning. For example, the French poet Benjamin Péret, the most extreme political insurrectionary of the Surrealists, and a Trotskyist, arrived in Barcelona within two days of the proletarian triumph.

Such marginal types were accompanied by rank-and-file socialdemocratic labourers and intellectuals from around Europe. Only the Communists held back, kept on a short leash by Moscow, until September, when Joseph Stalin issued an electrifying order to cadres around the world: "The Spanish conflict is not the affair of the Spaniards alone, but of all progressive humanity," he was credited with saying. The Soviet Union, a government ruling a sixth of the world, and the self-proclaimed vanguard of socialist revolution with one of the most powerful armies in the globe, would stand alongside the defenders of the Spanish Republic. Only the revolutionary government of Lázaro Cárdenas in Mexico offered similar assistance to the "loyalist" regime in Madrid.

Military units were hastily assembled in Russia and from among the German and other Communist exiles in Paris. Some recruits had served in the Red Army; many were veterans of trench fighting in World

War I. They first appeared in the streets of Madrid on the morning of Sunday, November 8, 1936 – the day after the 19th anniversary of the Bolshevik Revolution.

Their arrival could not have been more dramatic. Madrid was pounded by bombing planes and besieged by 20,000 rebel troops, with, in the front ranks of the attackers, Moroccan mercenaries known for their brutal atrocities, including mass rapes. Wave after wave of the rightist forces had advanced into the vulnerable south-western side of the city. The working-class women of Madrid were warned to prepare for individual resistance, to keep butcher knives and other simple implements of defence handy, to be ready to throw boiling oil on the invaders. Able-bodied men were ordered from their workplaces to the trenches. Meanwhile, the Republican government was evacuated to Valencia.

The night of November 7 was stormy, with rain drenching Madrid and lightning blasting open the sky. Civilians prepared for the imminent fall of the city and what would doubtless be a mad flight. Shelling induced residents to leave their apartment buildings, which they believed were targeted, and to attempt sleep under trees and benches along fashionable boulevards – hardly a safer alternative, but many had been unhinged by the siege. Foreign newspapers were reporting that Madrid had already fallen. A company of Socialist women volunteers was almost entirely wiped out, near midnight, in the chaos.

And then, in the misty dawn, with great discipline, some 1,700 "international" volunteers — Germans, Poles, French, and Italians — were seen on Madrid's main thoroughfare, the Gran Vía, in corduroy uniforms and steel helmets, carrying rifles and red flags. Crowds on the sidewalks applauded, cheered, and wept as the armed men marched by, singing revolutionary anthems. The newcomers joined the anarchist militia in the front lines. The enemy assault resumed, with the roar of artillery. But the defence held. Days later the "internationals" appeared again at the Bridge of the French, on the river Manzanares, famous in Spanish history as the place where fighters 120 years before had stopped Napoleon's troops. The Bridge of the French, which had almost been taken by the Moroccan *tabores*, was also held. And, temporarily, Madrid was saved.

Overnight, the "internationals" in Madrid were world heroes, and it became known that these units were created at Stalin's order. Their commander was the Soviet army general Emil Kleber, real name Moshe Stern, a Bukovinan Jew and, incredibly, former head of Soviet military intelligence in North America. The Madrileños had known the truth from the start, crying out, *"¡Vivan los rusos! ¡Aquí están los rusos!"* at first sight of the volunteers. They became the International Brigades (I.B.), an assemblage of de facto Soviet detachments within the Spanish Army, serving as a counterpart to the Foreign Legion under Franco, which had led the rebellion.

Back in New York, a clandestine directive to recruit young American Communists for service in Spain had been received during the same week in November. Among those selected for enlistment was Irving Weissman. When he got to Spain, he was assigned to the Canadian I.B. unit, the Mackenzie-Papineau Battalion. He was wounded, and returned to the United States when the I.B. were withdrawn from Spain by Stalin, late in 1938.

Mr. Weissman worked in shipyards in the United States until American entry into World War II, when he volunteered for the U.S. Army. He saw action in the invasion of Italy. After the war, he became a full-time employee of the Communist Party, first in upstate New York and later as executive secretary of the party in West Virginia.

In 1952, he was tried in Pennsylvania under the Smith Act, for conspiracy to advocate the overthrow of the U.S. government. However, a mistrial was declared, and Mr. Weissman served only a six-month sentence for contempt.

By that time, he had become disaffected with the party, which he considered rigid, doctrinaire and out of touch with American reality. He later worked in construction but remained active as a member of an International Brigades veterans' group.

He campaigned for the rights of Jewish veterans of the I.B. who suffered from the anti-Semitic policies of Poland's Communist secret police boss, Mieczyslaw Moczar, in the late 1960s. But he also supported the Sandinistas in Nicaragua.

In recent years, he was a member of the editorial board of *The Volunteer*, the official publication of American veterans of the Brigades.

All these details of a long and, from a certain perspective, a virtuous life, were included in the *Chronicle* obituary. But sadly, Irving Weissman's survivors were not left to grieve for him in peace. The day the obituary appeared, his daughter, and news editors at the daily paper, were deluged with angry telephone calls from the hard-line Stalinists among the veterans, rebuking Mr. Weissman's family and demanding a correction of a phrase in the obituary. His daughter was even assailed on the street by an angry former comrade.

The offending clause? "The brigades were ordered out of Spain by Joseph Stalin." As Dave Smith, "Bay Area post commander" of the "Veterans of the Abraham Lincoln Brigade [sic] and Associates," wrote to the *Chronicle* city editor, "This statement is a lie and is a perfect example of a cold-war red-baiting distortion of the Spanish civil war... We expect a correction to be published." According to these fanatics, the withdrawal of the I.B., announced on September 21, 1938, was a decision taken by the Spanish Republican authorities alone. Stalin, they declared, had nothing to do with it.

No correction was printed in the *San Francisco Chronicle*. But the controversy over so trivial a difference in interpretation exemplifies the most remarkable aspect of the Spanish war's impact in the United States. The conflict itself ended on April 1, 1939. Yet the war about the war – argument upon argument, frequently brutal and hurtful, over what happened and why – has yet to end.

II.

No correction of the *Chronicle* obituary for Irving Weissman was needed because, notwithstanding the political mythology perpetuated by sentimentalists, the I.B. were under the complete and absolute control of the Soviet government from top to bottom, from beginning to end. This was confirmed beyond doubt, after the fall of Soviet Communism, by the opening of the I.B. archives in, unsurprisingly, Moscow, and the publication of selected documents on the Brigades. Some of the most disturbing items were put in print in the U.S., in *The Secret World of American Communism*, edited by Harvey Klehr, John Earl Haynes and Fridrikh I. Firsov.

Furthermore, the truth about the I.B. withdrawal from Spain was perceived, at the time, by numerous Spanish and foreign observers.

Jesús Hernández, who had been a Communist minister in the Spanish Republican government, later wrote that Moscow "wished to deprive the Republic of any possibility of further resistance," because

Stalin, realizing that "all his diplomatic manoeuvres [to influence Britain and France] had been a resounding failure," had decided "to negotiate with Berlin, offering as proof of his sincerity the corpse of the Spanish Republic." Thus, while removing the International Brigades from Spain, Stalin attempted to maintain his influence through a puppet, Spanish Republican premier Juan Negrín.

Of course, as we know, less than a year after the announcement that the I.B. would leave Spain, the Stalin-Hitler pact had been signed in Moscow and the Nazis and Stalinists were preparing the 20th century partition of Poland.

Some I.B. volunteers, including Americans, had resisted the withdrawal order. For example, the modernist composer Conlon Nancarrow, who died in Mexico City in 1997, had joined the American Communist Party in 1934, and went to Europe as a jazz trumpeter aboard a pleasure ship in 1936. The next year, he enlisted in the I.B., serving in the Abraham Lincoln Battalion, made up of Americans, Cubans, and Spanish draftees.

Nancarrow's first published compositions, the "Toccata for Violin and Piano" and the "Prelude and Blues for Piano," were issued by Nicolas Slonimsky in 1938, while he was in Spain at the front. When the I.B. were evacuated, Nancarrow joined a Spanish-only unit and remained in combat. With the defeat of the Republic in 1939, he escaped from the port of Valencia by stowing away in a ship loaded with olive oil.

The debate over the Spanish war involves many more details than the withdrawal order, but all those that are subjects for acrimony today lead back to Stalin and Stalinism. That is in great part because in the aftermath of the conflict a deliberately falsified version of its history, concocted by Stalinist methods and under Soviet inspiration, was imposed on the consciousness of American liberals and radicals.

In this "official" legend, the Communists were the best fighters in Spain, the most competent and courageous; indeed, the war itself became less an episode in Spanish and European history than a chapter in the epic of American Communism – a bright and shining moment in which the Stalinist atrocities in the USSR were rendered moot. The Spanish people, it was said, made up songs about their Communist heroes – songs that, peculiarly enough, were rendered to

American audiences by such performers as Pete Seeger, playing a distinctly un-Spanish instrument, the banjo. The rest of the world had turned its back on Spain, the mythologists claimed, while Stalin, the American Communists, and their comrades put their lives on the line against the fascists, well ahead of those who made great and heroic sacrifices, after 1941, in World War II.

The official legend would include, in addition to its banjo tunes, other bizarre strictures about Spanish reality. The Spanish anarchists, whose ranks were two million strong, and who fought the war all the way to the end before a quarter million of them took refuge with their families in France, were portrayed, in a purported contrast with the Communists that was anything but coincidental, as fools and cowards. The anarchists had lost the war, according to Communist supporters, by their incessant indiscipline.

In addition, a smaller revolutionary force, the Partit Obrer d'Unificació Marxista (Workers' Party of Marxist Unification) or P.O.U.M., largely based in Catalonia, had turned against the Republic, according to the orthodox Stalinists, and joined the fascists – thus proving the accusations presented in the Moscow Trials that Trotsky, the reputed inspirer of the P.O.U.M., had hired himself out to Hitler.

Lastly, according to the myth, the war was only about fascism, about resisting Hitler's drive for world conquest. Arguments by isolated and irresponsible extremists, who said the war was really an expression of a social revolutionary crisis in Spain, were irrelevant – worse, such diversionary propaganda "objectively" helped Franco. And even more obscure and abstruse claims that the Spanish war involved the one and only instance of a near-successful working-class revolution in Western Europe, in keeping with Western democratic and populist traditions, did not merit being heard, much less answered.

Almost from the beginning this myth had its challengers. The most famous, of course, is George Orwell, whose *Homage to Catalonia* first appeared late in 1938. Orwell had not waited for a Muscovite invitation to support the Spanish left. Furthermore, he had enlisted in the P.O.U.M. militia, and had been seriously wounded in fighting on the Aragón front. And finally, he had witnessed a Communist attempt to outlaw the anarchists and P.O.U.M., in Barcelona in May 1937.

Denying such unpleasant realities as Orwell described was a major task for the Communist loyalists, but one to which they applied themselves with great dedication. Orwell was regularly trashed by Lincoln Battalion veterans, orally and in print. The 1996 release of a feature film, *Land and Freedom*, made by the leftist producer-director Ken Loach but following the anti-Stalinist line of Orwell, was met by horrified denunciations on the part of the "Lincolns," as they had come to nickname themselves, or "brigadistas," as their younger enthusiasts preferred to call them.

And of all the contested elements in this tapestry, none is more painful and provocative than the point made by Orwell and underlined in Loach's film: that the American and other foreign volunteers ended up as counter-revolutionary mercenaries used against the Spanish people. Not even the long-known execution of American volunteers as "deserters" is so traumatic to the guardians of the official version.

A whole new uproar broke out with publication of a memoir, *Jumping the Line: The Adventures and Misadventures of an American Radical*, by William Herrick. Herrick, a Communist cadre member from New York, had been sent to Spain and became an officer of a renowned machine gun company – an elite assignment – in the Lincoln Battalion. Wounded and repatriated, Herrick returned to the United States with a bullet in his neck, which was never removed.

But Herrick had already seen too much in Spain, and when he got back to New York he was buffeted by a new shock in the form of the Stalin-Hitler pact. He turned against the Communist Party altogether, and, disabled from his war wound, spent the rest of his life fighting slander and harassment from his former comrades.

His memoir was riveting and grim. *Jumping the Line* is, simply, the best account of the Spanish war ever published by an American volunteer. It is a thorough autopsy on the murdered idealism of the young Communists who went to fight the fascists in Spain but who, as Herrick showed, served as secret police thugs for Stalin against the anarchists, P.O.U.M., and anti-Soviet Socialists. It also shows – with a depth of understanding that revealed how deep were Herrick's own radical convictions – that the native supporters of the Spanish left were out for more than just a repudiation of "fascist" aggression: they were, to repeat, fighting for a social revolution, based on the labour movement, of a kind Stalin hated and feared much more than he did the Nazis.

Jumping the Line finally stood as a uniquely truthful and beautiful account of the lives of American and international Communist cadres in the Stalin era; Bill Herrick spoke for every comrade who risked his or her life fighting for the world revolution in the 1930s, only to be betrayed by Moscow. It is extremely doubtful that a better book about the appeal of revolutionary Communism or the experience of its youthful militants will ever be written, at least in English.

However, Herrick's relentless demolition of the legends of the Lincoln Battalion was not limited to a criticism of Stalin, or even of the secret, guilt about which clearly oppressed Herrick for years, that the foreigners had been employed to kill Spanish radical dissidents. In excruciating detail, Herrick showed that the American volunteers, most of them college boys or feckless young Communists from places like Brooklyn, without the war experience of the German, French, Belgian, Italian, and Slavic volunteers, went into battle after training that was criminally inadequate; that they were therefore slaughtered en masse; that they rebelled against the commissars and commanders who sacrificed and purged them, and that they even slew one of their officers, an American Black named Oliver Law, on the battlefield.

Much of this was originally spelt out by Herrick in a powerful novel, ¡*Hermanos!*, published in 1969, and was reiterated in the mid-1980s in interviews with the writer Paul Berman, then of the *Village Voice*. Berman recalled the brouhaha that erupted, complete with a "Lincoln" picket line at the *Voice* office and demands for his dismissal, in his preface to *Jumping the Line*.

The reaction to *Jumping the Line* from the Stalin-nostalgics was therefore predictable.

In the November 2, 1998 issue of *The Nation*, book reviewer John L. Hess served as designated hit-man for the Stalin lobby. Recycling an 11-year old *Nation* column, Hess declared that Herrick had "defamed" Oliver Law. Herrick, Hess charged, had borrowed the story of Law's death from the long-forgotten leftist and Bohemian novelist and screenwriter Bernard Wolfe; that Wolfe had heard it, like Herrick, from witnesses, was beyond Hess's imagining. Hess, determined to perform in the prescribed manner, wrote of Herrick and Law, "The deconstruction of radical heroes was enjoying a small boom. Writers were confirming the guilt of Tom Mooney, Joe Hill, Sacco and Vanzetti (whose crime is affirmed by a dead source in Herrick's memoir), the Rosenbergs and Alger Hiss."

Hess created this amalgamated list of radical victims at least partially out of his own fevered mind, since nobody has seriously claimed Mooney was guilty for eight decades, nor have any recent such claims been made about Joe Hill or Bartolomeo Vanzetti (Sacco is another matter.) And it should be apparent that Mooney, Hill, and Sacco and Vanzetti, who whatever their faults or crimes were authentic radicals, are dishonoured by being lumped in with Stalinist spies like the Rosenbergs and Hiss.

Hess's polemic was monumentally mean-spirited. "Herrick's second-hand accounts of disaster, which he attributes to Stalinist malignancy, could be transposed to any war," he declaimed. "That's war."

This despicable argument was answered, unexpectedly, in a letter to *The Nation* (November 30, 1998) from impeccably-radical columnist Todd Gitlin, who demanded to know what other wars had seen such incidents, described by Herrick, as "[t]he Communist assassination of three Spanish non-Communist leftists, witnessed by Herrick? A Comintern agent's gun muzzle pointed at Herrick because he's been heard making inconvenient remarks? The unexplained disappearance of a troublesome militant?"

III.

For a serious historian of the Spanish war, two aspects of this controversy stand out.

First is the arrogance of the "Lincolns," exceptional even in the mammoth lie factory operated by the American intellectual left, regarding their version of the Spanish past. Any other Americans who conducted themselves with such heedless self-righteousness regarding the culture and history of a foreign people would be considered clueless imperialists at best.

Pete Seeger's banjo versions of Spanish songs, with their lyrics typically altered to conform to the Party line, are a uniquely appropriate metonym for the overall character of American Communist memory about the war.

For the Spanish war, in the view of the "Lincolns" and their acolytes, was and remains about Americans, not about Spaniards. It is astonishing to realize that of the vast stream of memoirs and histories of the volunteers published by the "official" faction, not one –

not a single one – contains a useful review of the Spanish background of the war, to say nothing of a new contribution to Spanish historiography. It is as if Spain were an island somewhere in the Atlantic, to which the "Lincolns" were transported in a hermetically-sealed capsule, and from which they were returned to the company of their comrades in Brooklyn.

However, this indifference to the previous experience of the Spaniards the "Lincolns" had allegedly come to assist – expressed, above all, in the failure of most of them to learn any Spanish at all, as I found out at the beginning of my research on the war, 35 years ago – reflected, in the end, a central fact about the Spanish experience.

The "Lincoln" volunteers had come from an American radical milieu in which the Communist Party, however small and isolated, was by far the dominant element; in addition, youthful American radicals of the '30s were amazingly susceptible to the triumphalist attitude of the Stalinists, who claimed to be creating a "new man" that embodied history as none ever had before. But Spain was wholly different; there the Communist Party, notwithstanding the propaganda campaign to build up such figures as Dolores Ibarruri, known as La Pasionaria, was a small and unpopular sect, without roots in the country's labour history.

Spanish revolutionary politics had been dominated for several generations by the long-established mass movements of the anarchists and Socialists, alongside which the Stalinist Communists offered a pretty meagre profile. That the entire Communist effort was financed from abroad was distasteful to Spanish workers; and most importantly, nearly all the founders of the Spanish Communist Party, who were sincere and experienced revolutionaries, had broken with Moscow after Stalin's accession to power, and by 1936 were to be found in the ranks of the P.O.U.M. With the onset of Stalin's intervention, Soviet arms, political influence, and the arrival of secret police (N.K.V.D.) cadres on Spanish territory induced some Republican military officers, state bureaucrats, ambitious intellectuals, and other opportunists into the ranks of the Communist Party. But the Party never gained the wide constituency and intense loyalty and affection enjoyed by their anarchist and other rivals.

In the absence of a Spanish Communist tradition in which they could orient themselves, it was doubtless understandable that the

"Lincolns" would come to view the Spaniards themselves from a distance and with a disdain not much different from the feeling of most American troops toward their Southeast Asian battle comrades 30 years later. Like the "Lincolns," few Americans in Vietnam learned the language or the history of the places in which they were risking their lives.

More difficult to understand is why, apparently, no new historical understanding penetrated the armoured memory of the surviving "Lincolns" and their supporters, even with the passage of 60 years. It was as if, once back from a Spain they never knew, they had been intellectually trapped in amber. But the most amazing aspect of this wilful ignorance, and of the rivalries over history that we still witness, is that, all unknown to the "Lincolns," the battle of historical memory has been won in Spain itself. No, not by the Francoists, who won the shooting war, but who even now have few advocates; rather, the ideological war was won by the anti-Communist left.

Thus, in a phenomenon that mirrors the sought-for monopoly of the "Lincolns" over writing and publishing about the Spanish war in the U.S., a fascinating development took place in Spain after the death of dictator Franco in 1975. Of hundreds of volumes of memoirs, biography, analysis, and research that have appeared in the Spanish, Catalan, and Basque languages over the past quarter century, almost none defend the reputation of the Communists, the intervention of the Soviet Union, or the broader Stalinist interpretation of the war. The speeches of forgotten Socialist leaders have been reprinted; every tiny commune of anarchist peasants seems to have seen its activities memorialised; a considerable library of P.O.U.M. literature has been republished, with many recent additions to its bibliography. But there are few, if any, volumes glorifying La Pasionaria, or the International Brigades. Indeed, the Muscovite claim that there was nothing at stake in Spain but democracy vs. international fascist aggression is almost completely absent from the Spanish historical discourse, in which the conflict of the 1930s is typically referred to as *"la revolución."*

This is a matter on which Spanish historians of both the right and the left tend to agree. To all of them, the war was the outcome of a profound upheaval that had gestated in Spain for more than 100 years, based in the land question, the issue of lay education, the corruption of the monarchy and the military, and the legacy of Castilian centralism, complicated by the growth of an aggressive labour movement and the emergence of a modern nationalism among the peripheral ethnicities.

If they disagree it is over whether the Franco counter-revolution was justified; and most of today's Spanish historians, like those in the U.S., define themselves as of the left. But nobody in Spain, apart from a handful of old Stalinists, defends the Communist line. And everybody knows that Stalin betrayed the republic; the P.O.U.M. founder Joaquím Maurín argued that the Spanish Republic was defeated as soon as it became clear to the Spanish people that the war in which they were fighting had become a conflict between Franco and Stalin. They were ready to fight Franco to the death; but not for the benefit of Dzhugashvili. Even the final manoeuvres of the Communists, when the collapse of the Republic was unavoidable, in demanding continued resistance and accusing all who thought of a negotiated surrender as traitors, were and are seen as what they were: evil efforts to continue speculating in Spanish blood for the profit of Stalinism.

The "Lincolns" may claim that their version of history was legitimised by a recent decision of the Spanish government to award the surviving veterans a highly-conditional option of citizenship. But the long delay in granting this status, which was proposed many years ago, and the political intrigues that accompanied it, were so baroque as to somewhat deflate the honour.

That the battle of historical memory was won in Spain by the anti-Stalinists is visible in many ways and places. One is the existence of a *plaça* named for George Orwell near the Barcelona waterfront; that was made possible by the mayoral administration of Pasqual Maragall, of the Catalan Socialist Party. Another is the inauguration, in Can Rull, a Catalan town with a Communist mayor, of a street named for Andreu Nin.

Recollection of the terrible death of the P.O.U.M. leader Nin, assassinated by Soviet secret police agents in the summer of 1937, at age 45, has a special place in this process. In the late 1970s, with the Francoist regime dismantled and radical spirits in revival, it became common to hear in Spain that the civil war had been fought between "the (rightwing) killers of Federico García Lorca and the murderers of Andreu Nin." In recent years, to a handful of foreigners, especially admirers of Orwell, Nin's case involved a fading echo of a tragic, internecine struggle within the Spanish drama, but little else. In Catalonia it meant quite a bit more.

Nin, born in El Vendrell, the same Catalan locale as the cellist Pau (Pablo) Casals, was a great deal more than the head of a minor "Trotskyist" party. He had also been a leading figure in the anarchosyndicalist labour movement in Barcelona in the 1920s; implicated in a major terrorist conspiracy, he had fled to the Soviet Union. In Moscow, he married a Russian woman and rose to a high position in the international Communist network, but then became a Trotskyist and was sent into internal exile. The saga of Nin's escape from Stalin and his return to Barcelona in 1930 was extensively covered by the Spanish daily press.

But more importantly, Nin had been a successful journalist and essayist, contributing to literary periodicals with the greatest influence in the Catalan cultural revival before and during World War I. This fact might have guaranteed him no more than a footnote in anthologies and manuals issued in an obscure Romance idiom, were it not for his skill as a translator from Russian into Catalan. After his fall from authority in Moscow, and with his return to Catalonia, Nin had made his living translating and publishing Russian novels.

The effects of this professional decision were varied. On one hand, we now know that the martyrdom of the Russian novelist Boris Pilnyak (1894-1937), one of that country's outstanding 20th century writers, was at least partially caused by the unfortunate fact that Pilnyak's 1930 volume, *The Volga Flows into the Caspian,* had been done into Catalan by Nin. Pilnyak had kept letters from Nin that were, fatally, found by the N.K.V.D.

But Nin's Russian translations also made possible a posthumous revenge on the Stalinists. In the 1960s, after the Franco regime lifted its ban on Catalan-language secondary education, thousands of young Catalans read Nin's translation of Dostoyevsky's *Crime and Punishment,* as part of their regular literature courses. Nin also translated *Anna Karenina* and works by Chekhov and Zoshchenko, as well as, of course, Trotsky. In addition, several Catalan writers published reminiscences of him — among other things, it has been revealed that he had been the lover of the highly popular Catalan woman novelist Mercè Rodoreda. And everyone who read his translations or heard about him learned that he had been tortured and executed by Stalin's agents.

Today, my coauthor Víctor Alba, one of Nin's three main biographers, lectures continually around the Catalan circuit, on the Stalinist persecution of the P.O.U.M. and the death of Nin.

The historiographic victory of the anti-Stalinists on Spanish territory is reflected in other facts. A Welsh-born Jew, Burnett Bolloten, who died in 1987, emerged as the authoritative historian of the war, in Spanish even more than English, in a position comparable with that of Robert Conquest regarding the history of Stalin's repression. As a United Press correspondent on the Republican side in the Spanish war, Bolloten had observed a great deal, and as a former Communist with associations in the N.K.V.D., he learned even more. In 1940 he found himself in Mexico, ordered by his Communist superiors to join the plot against Trotsky. He refused and broke with the Soviets, beginning an odyssey that would lead him to write *The Spanish Civil War: Revolution and Counterrevolution*, a huge study published in 1991. Bolloten's judgement is the same as Herrick's, and as that shared by millions of Spaniards: that Stalin deliberately manipulated, betrayed, and helped destroy the Spanish Republic.

IV.

The opening of archives was naturally important for the recovery of the Spanish truth. Thanks to Nikita Khrushchev, it had been fully established that the vast majority of Soviet officers who had been sent to Spain, including such once-famous individuals as Moshe Stern, had been massacred in the purges just before World War II. Indeed, it was obvious that for Stalin the very fact of having served in Spain, so far from the Soviet borders, made such personnel highly suspect. In addition, numerous high-ranking Communist veterans of the Spanish war had been purged in Eastern Europe after World War II, and, in the 1960s and 1970s, most of their reputations were restored, and the files on their cases opened, in such countries as Czechoslovakia and Hungary. It was then partly disclosed, as well, that rumours about purges and mass executions in the Slavic and Hungarian detachments of the I.B. were true.

Even before the great revelations from the Russian archives, after 1991, significant documentation on the war and the Soviet intervention in it had come to light in Spain. With the fall of the Republican administration in 1939, vast files had been seized by the Franco forces, and came to be housed in the National Historical Archives in Salamanca and Madrid. They were preserved and catalogued until the late 1980s, when they were made available to scholars.

The Spanish documents comprise many of considerable use to historians like Bolloten, such as copies of reports in Russian, from Soviet agents on the scene, to Moscow. But one very thick file was outstandingly important: the transcripts from the 1938 trial of the P.O.U.M., charged at Soviet insistence with "high treason and espionage" against the Republic. Among the subsidiary entries was a series of notes prepared for the N.K.V.D. interrogation of the P.O.U.M. defendants and other suspects. And one sheet of comments had to do with none other than Eric Blair, i.e. George Orwell.

This document has been printed in English in the *Complete Works of George Orwell*, edited by the unfortunate Peter Davison. However, it is accompanied therein by inaccurate comments showing that Davison and his collaborators on that project did not comprehend what it was and what it means. Davison was also responsible for an earlier example of intellectual vandalism, the issuance of an "edited" version of *Homage to Catalonia* that contributed nothing but confusion to Orwell studies.

The N.K.V.D. notes on Orwell are found in a batch of reports on foreigners involved with the P.O.U.M., most of whom were arrested and at least two of whom were killed. These "assessments" were produced by the State Special Information Department, a Communist-controlled Spanish police body. The notations on Orwell are slender but ominous. The original memorandum is dated July 13, 1937, three weeks after Orwell escaped from Spain, but the matter was kept active until November 26, 1937, the date of a cover letter attached to it.

Orwell and his wife Eileen were, first of all, described in the secret police memorandum as "pronounced Trotskyists" on the basis of their correspondence. They were also said to be members of the British Independent Labour Party (I.L.P.), in whose "committee" on the Aragón front Orwell was alleged to have functioned. A sinister cast was given, in the notes, to a credential signed by Georges Kopp, Orwell's commander in the P.O.U.M. militia and later his relative by marriage, whom he tried to rescue from Communist detention in Barcelona, as described in *Homage to Catalonia*. The credential was analysed as a safe-conduct for the use of Eileen Blair during the May

1937 street fighting in the city, which is, of course, the centrepiece of *Homage*. The charge of possessing clandestine or subversive credentials was evidence of a clear intent by Stalin's agents to liquidate the British author.

In addition, the document also includes a cryptic, but deadly notation, "Contact with Moscow," referring to the Blair couple. It is absurd to think that Orwell in Spain had contacts in Moscow; but it is not absurd to conceive of the Stalinist police fabricating such links in the interest of a Moscow-style trial. Indeed, the surviving comrades of Andreu Nin always believed that the Soviet assault on the P.O.U.M. was motivated by the belief that a "Moscow trial" could be organized outside Soviet borders, to dispel the doubts about the show proceedings that had been voiced by many foreign liberals and leftists. Nin, they say, obstructed such a project by giving up his life rather than to falsely confess; his death, they say, saved the rest of them.

In chapter 13 of *Homage to Catalonia*, Orwell rather light-heartedly mentioned that, after he had gone into hiding during the Stalinist raids in Barcelona, his correspondence had been seized by Communist agents from his wife's hotel room. The document I have cited clearly originated with the N.K.V.D. examination of that sequestered archive. But Orwell himself somewhat downplayed the interest in him shown by Stalin's minions, writing simply, "I was not guilty of any definite act, but I was guilty of 'Trotskyism.' The fact that I had served in the P.O.U.M. militia was quite enough to get me into prison."

In reality and in the context of the cited document, this comment seems both an exaggeration and an understatement. Firstly, the document contains much more about his presence in Barcelona than about his militia service at the Aragón front. By and large, P.O.U.M. militia service alone was not enough to result in the arrest of any person, even a foreigner. The P.O.U.M. and its militia included tens of thousands of people serving at the front, in Catalan local governments, and on the borders of the Republican state, until the war ended. Even the Stalinists were not reckless or confident enough to directly confront such a force. Thus, although a group of German volunteers was seized in the Stalinist repression described by Orwell, and the Stalinists continued arresting and even murdering individual P.O.U.M. militia members throughout the war, few anti-Stalinists in Spain were persecuted only for a P.O.U.M. militia affiliation.

However, the Soviets were definitely intent on decapitating the P.O.U.M. and destroying its leadership, and the involvement of any individual, Spanish or foreign, with the top political stratum of the P.O.U.M. was an extremely serious matter. The document I have discussed identifies Orwell as the liaison between the P.O.U.M. and the British I.L.P. Thus, Orwell's correspondence, indicating to the N.K.V.D. that he was a prominent foreign supporter of the P.O.U.M. rather than a rank-and-file militia member, would have made him eligible for disappearance and execution, not simply imprisonment. That, in fact, was exactly the fate of Orwell's counterpart, an Austrian dissident Marxist named Kurt Landau who functioned as the P.O.U.M.'s liaison to German-speaking anti-Stalinist groups. Landau was kidnapped by Soviet agents in Barcelona and disappeared; his arrest order surfaced in the Salamanca files.

In general those foreigners arrested in the early N.K.V.D. raids on the P.O.U.M. were revolutionary hangers-on who stayed in Barcelona, frequenting political meetings and gossiping. Orwell's preference for life at the front, rather than as an ideological gadfly back in the city, probably saved him. So long as he was at the front the Franco troops might kill him, but he was out of Stalinist reach.

But after May 1937 Orwell was not completely safe anywhere behind the Spanish Republican lines. He modestly presented himself in *Homage to Catalonia* as a fairly unsophisticated and obscure individual when he went to Spain. In reality, he was publicly hailed on his arrival there, by the P.O.U.M. An unsigned notice on Orwell, headed, "British Author With the Militia," appeared in an English-language P.O.U.M. bulletin, *Spanish Revolution,* in February 1937, and his photograph, in the company of Nin and others, was printed elsewhere in the P.O.U.M. press. Such publicity unquestionably made him a major target of the N.K.V.D., yet, in his characteristically self-effacing way, he never disclosed just how great a danger he had faced in Barcelona.

The Spanish archival revelations have been complemented, of course, by Soviet documentary releases. One of the first and most important such disclosures came when TV3, the Barcelona-based Catalan-language television network, sent a team of reporters to Moscow, where they were able to obtain the operational file on the killing of Nin. Their investigation resulted in a documentary, *Operation Nikolai* – titled after the codename used by the N.K.V.D. for him –

shown in 1992 on prime time in Catalonia, then in the rest of Spain, and finally on national television in France.

Operation Nikolai traces the life and death of Nin step by step, and includes several unambiguous statements. Pelai Pagès, a left-wing biographer of Nin, pictured in the courtyard of the University of Barcelona where he teaches, declared without flourishes, "The assassination of Andreu Nin signified the assassination of the Spanish revolution." A veteran anarchist, Juan Liarte, was more vehement: "Stalin was afraid of our revolution!" he declared. "Stalin had to destroy our revolution!"

Nowhere in the Catalan TV film is the Lincoln Battalion mentioned; nor was La Pasionaria, who appeared briefly, even identified. One can imagine the wave of apoplexies that would sweep the "Lincolns" and their admirers if such a documentary were to be shown on prime-time TV in America.

Another rebuke to the official Communist version of the Spanish war came a year later, in 1993, with publication of *Deadly Illusions,* by John Costello and Oleg Tsarev. This volume, a biography of the mysterious N.K.V.D. "defector" Lev Lazarevich Feldbin, alias Orlov, included much on the Nin murder, which Orlov, as N.K.V.D. boss in Spain, coordinated, before his "defection" to the U.S. in 1938. The previously-mentioned selection of documents from the Comintern archives, *The Secret World of American Communism,* included definitive evidence on the iron control over the I.B. exercised by the N.K.V.D., with deadly results for alleged "deserters," Americans included.

The U.S. National Security Agency's publication of the Venona papers also contributed to an accurate record about Spain. Of some 2,900 N.K.V.D. messages sent during World War II and thereafter, many, originating in New York, San Francisco, and Mexico City, showed the continued use of Spanish Republican political figures and I.B. veterans, with Americans naturally among them, as N.K.V.D. agents. One such individual was Victori Salà, a key Russian-controlled provocateur in the fraudulent treason case for which the P.O.U.M. was tried. Sala, who showed up in Mexico City, and whose codename or *klichka* was "Jota," or "J," was described in an N.K.V.D. communication dated June 29, 1944, in chilling terms: "Please look into the question of bringing J into our work here on the polecats [Trotskyists] and of setting up a group for tracing people and for external surveillance, for which there is a great need."

Clearly, the murderous campaign against anti-Stalinist leftists, carried out in Spain against Nin, Orwell, and others, and which William Herrick alone has described as an American insider, continued long afterward, and far away.

If the structure of Stalinist lies has collapsed in Spain itself, it may also be said that cracks have appeared in the edifice the "Lincolns" erected in the American historical consciousness. The publication of Herrick's *Jumping the Line* represented a major such fissure. That deep within the system of falsehoods, other weaknesses exist is proven by the posthumous report of Irving Weissman's fight for honesty among the American I.B. veterans. For, according to his survivors, Irving Weissman had tried for years to introduce a breath of historic fresh air into the cramped, stuffy parlour of the "Lincolns."

But the struggle for truth continues, as demonstrated by the angry response to the Weissman obituary in the *San Francisco Chronicle*. Obviously, some of the "Lincolns" and their fans will never change. However, the American historian Ronald Radosh, at the time of publication of the present work, was preparing a volume on Spain drawn from the records of the Soviet military and secret police. Radosh also utilised the newly-released Mask documents, some tens of thousands of decrypted communications between Moscow and Comintern agents abroad, including in Spain, which have been made public in Britain by MI6. Unfortunately, Radosh, whose real competence in studying the war was limited, had tended to defend the thesis that a Franco triumph was preferable to a Communist victory.

But that is a false duality: notwithstanding the argument of Maurín, and the perceptions of many that the war had become a contest between Franco and Stalin, it was not. The N.K.V.D. and other Soviet agents never attained full control over the Republican regime; thus, the Spanish Tribunal for High Treason and Espionage failed to find the P.O.U.M. guilty of such charges. That is why Stalin's order for the withdrawal of the I.B. remains so sensitive an issue; it shows that Stalin contributed directly to the Republican defeat, and indicates the greatest lesson of all, known to millions of Spaniards then and now: that the war against Franco could only be won if it had also been a war against the Communists.

And what, then, should our verdict? That men like Irving

Weissman, Moshe Stern, and Conlon Nancarrow, like Orwell and William Herrick, were heroes, in fighting for the Spanish Republic? Unquestionably. That the Spanish people were right in refusing to fight for Stalin? Unarguably. That the majority of those who fought to the end did so against Stalin and Stalinism? For Spaniards, that debate, too, is settled – to the discredit of Moscow and its acolytes. Yet, sadly, the battle over history, won in Spain by the anti-Stalinists, remains far from a victory for truth, in the land where Abraham Lincoln was born.

–Presented to VIth World Congress, International Council for Central and East European Studies, Tampere, Finland, July-August 2000

A Spectre Is Haunting Bosnia

Sarajevo, Bosnia-Herzegovina

The evening of May 3, 2000, saw the opening of a photographic retrospective here in the capital of Bosnia-Herzegovina. It was a beautiful night, if a little cool. Waiters circulated among the public at the Collegium Artisticum, a local gallery, offering drinks and hors d'oeuvres. The crowd was large.

The exhibit, "Tito in Bosnia-Herzegovina, 1943-1980" was held on the eve of the 20th anniversary of the Yugoslav dictator's demise. Clearly many, if not all, of the spectators, remained in mourning for him.

The images in the room began with photos of a young, macho Tito fighting the Germans in World War II and ended with portraits of an old, obese man who had to be helped from his limousine. The late dictator was always imposing, but the one facial characteristic he maintained throughout his life was a kind of involuntary sneer. At the beginning, it seemed as if he might be snarling derisively at the Nazis. At the end, he resembled nothing so much as a Mafia don who has grown very, very tired of his cronies and his burdensome responsibilities.

In case one missed the message of the exhibit, the headlines Sarajevo papers carried the next day made the point clear: "We lived better then." This longing for the past is preventing a better future.

Among elderly Bosnians it is common to hear the litany of nostalgia: there was no unemployment then, wages were high, a Yugoslav passport was recognized everywhere in the world. The Tito commemorations that week included a TV broadcast of the film *Sutjeska*, in which he was portrayed by none other than Richard Burton, and even a reprint of a 1946 profile from *Time* magazine.

One can hardly impugn the feelings of those who saw the relatively civilised world of Titoite Communism crumble into a jungle of ethnic massacres, as Yugoslavia did under the direction of Tito's successors. But there is something outrageous about the Tito cult in Bosnia-Herzegovina. For Tito's rule did much to prepare the ground for the Yugoslav horror. His *"L'État, c'est moi"* approach left the inevitable *"Aprés moi, le deluge"* effect. And the deluge was called Slobodan Milošević.

Tito was not all bad, to be sure. Like the Spanish *generalísimo*, Francisco Franco, he held the lid on his country for some 35 years, but allowed citizens to work abroad. Both created tourist industries that should make Fidel Castro envious.

But there the comparisons diverge. Franco took a Spain that, in 1936, resembled a senile grandmother dying of cancer, and left us, to extend the metaphor, a beautiful young girl. Franco was brutal in his prosecution of the Spanish civil war, but so were his opponents. And Franco never massacred people tens of thousands at a time, as Tito's Partisan forces did in the aftermath of the infamous Bleiburg events of 1945. Indeed, as a good Communist, Tito engaged in one practice unknown under Francoism: he killed his own comrades. The intelligent, liberal Croat Communist Andrija Hebrang, much beloved among his people, was murdered and slandered as an alleged Soviet spy.

This does not mean that Franco's side necessarily deserved to win the Spanish war; nor that it would have been better for Tito to lose the Partisan struggle. History is not static; individuals and circumstances change. The Franco against whom George Orwell risked his life in battle proved beneficial for Spain, but few, in retrospect, would want to side against Orwell.

Above all, one could never imagine a Madrid event honouring Franco attracting leading intellectuals of the kind who showed up on May 3 in Sarajevo to affirm their loyalty to Tito. Bosnia's answer to

Alessandra Mussolini, Svetlana Broz, the dictator's granddaughter, paraded around the photo show like a prom queen. La Mussolini is constantly abused in the Italian and foreign press, while Dr. Broz is adulated by many Bosnians.

And, of course, Franco provided for a rational succession (picking, in fact, the head of state that Spain still has, King Juan Carlos). And 20 years dead, Tito, again unlike Franco, continues to interfere. The Tito who electrified the world with his courage in facing down Stalin in 1948 proved so dominating a father figure that he has left a great many of his Bosnian and other ex-Yugoslav inheritors in a state of childish dependency. This, not the alleged corruption of Muslim politicians in Sarajevo, is the reason why the Bosnian economy is at a standstill.

What accounts for this? Journalists, of course, tend to be left-leaning all over the world, so it's not surprising that Tito has received better press than, say, Franco. This holds true for both dictators inside as well as outside their respective countries.

Secondly, and much more importantly, the "international community" running Bosnia feeds these delusions. The foreign authorities who hold the future of Bosnia-Herzegovina in their hands have made it abundantly clear that to them, a Titoite restoration in Bosnia, in the form of an electoral takeover by former Communist cadres who now call themselves Social Democrats, would be just fine. In recent municipal elections the official administrators of Bosnia-Herzegovina – including the Office of the High Representative, Wolfgang Petritsch, and the local legates of the Organization for Security and Cooperation in Europe – openly advocated a Social Democratic victory, referring to the party of the former dictatorship as "moderate and multiethnic."

One reason for this is that, perhaps understandably, the foreign authorities in Sarajevo have made a fetish out of opposing nationalism. To them, Bosnia has no future, only a past, and like the ex-Communists, the foreigners view that past with nostalgia. After all, there was peace, and Bosnians were not ethnically segregated.

But in Bosnia today (almost eerily like Spain on the eve of war in 1936), there is no liberal option; There are only "Whites" and "Reds" if you will. The "Social Democrats" are certainly not liberal. They are still Marxist in their habits, and not very moderate about it. Yes, of course, they're multiethnic – they are the former *nomenklatura*, which had to be multiethnic to run the country.

Zlatko Lagumdzija, the young computer expert who heads the Social Democrats, even has a strong physical resemblance to Tito. He has been designated by the foreign powers in Bosnia-Herzegovina to become the country's next president. He was at the exhibit, of course. He circulated around the photographs with a pleased grin. After all, he knows that his fellow-citizens consider a vote for him a vote for Tito.

Unfortunately, however, continued meddling by the dead hand of Tito means stagnation and poverty in Bosnia-Herzegovina for a long, long time.

–The Wall Street Journal Europe, May 17, 2000

* * * * *

Moscow and the Italian Communist Party

Remember the Italian Communist Party's famous break with the Soviet Union, its embrace of NATO, its moderation, its "Eurocommunism?" Guess what. The whole thing was orchestrated from Moscow.

Why should we care? Well, the Soviet Union has only been dead a decade, and revisionism is already beginning to creep up here and there. And communism itself is still alive and keeping in former backwaters of the empire such as Cuba, Vietnam and North Korea. In Italy itself, a former Communist was prime minister until a few weeks ago.

In Italy Communism achieved a level of support unknown elsewhere in Western Europe (one could say rather, the highest independently confirmed level of support in the universe) largely due to the superstar status of Enrico Berlinguer, the long-time Italian Communist leader. In 1976, when he was at the height of his popularity, an Italian movie came out titled *Berlinguer, I Love You*, that included the acting debut of none other than Roberto Benigni, Italy's Oscar-winning star. Berlinguer was quite an actor himself. But he preferred a different kind of role from those that Mr. Benigni played.

The Communist politician performed for the world as a born-again democrat and even free marketeer. According to the official story, he had led his massive party, the largest Communist movement in the West, to break with Moscow in 1976, the year in which love for him was proclaimed on the silver screen. His very biography seemed to lend itself to this role.

Mr. Berlinguer was born in Sassari, Sardinia, in 1922, to a landowning family that some described as aristocratic. At his death in 1984, *The New York Times* claimed he had been an acquaintance of Antonio Gramsci, the former Mussolini supporter who helped found the Italian Communist movement and later became an intellectual icon throughout the West. But Berlinguer would have had to have made Gramsci's acquaintance under exceptional circumstances – since Gramsci died, after a long spell in prison, when Berlinguer was in his teens, and years before he became a Communist.

Berlinguer carefully laid the groundwork for his party's rise to prominence. In 1973 he began a makeover of his movement with an eye toward increasing its acceptability to Italian voters and Italy's NATO partners, the so-called "historic compromise." The Italian Communists announced that they had abandoned revolution and would attempt a coalition with the then-dominant Christian Democrats.

Berlinguer remained a minor figure on the world stage until 1976, when on the eve of election he publicly acclaimed NATO and its nuclear shield, behind which he professed to feel "safer" as an Italian and fan of democracy. Europe and much of the rest of the world marvelled: Italy had produced a new, independent form of Communism, it was said. The Italian had outdone Marshal Tito and Chairman Mao in affirming that Communism was not a monolithic affair directed from the Soviet Union after all.

And the bet paid off. Italian Communists gained 34.4 per cent of the vote. It was the closest the Italian Communists ever came to real power. After 1976, Italian communism metastasised as "Eurocommunism." Partly bankrolled by none other than Romanian Communist dictator Nicolae Ceausescu, it also took over the communist parties of Spain, Finland, and other European countries.

But we now have compelling evidence that it was all a lie. Last month, historian R. Gualtieri held a seminar at the Gramsci Institute, which belongs to the formerly Communist Party that now likes to style itself the Party of the Democratic Left. An excerpt from the paper he presented was printed in nothing less than *L'Unità*, the former official organ of the Communist Party. In it, Mr. Gualtieri lets the cat out of the bag.

"Berlinguer's famous interview (in 1976) did not in any way constitute a break with the Soviet Union," Gualtieri said. The Moscow party leadership gave his moves the green light, he added.

Any educated observer of communism also realizes that Berlinguer also lied handily about his — and his party's — past. In the 1970s, he claimed he and his comrades "never believed that one single party, or single class, can solve the problems of our country," as recalled in *The New York Times'* obituary for him. This breathtaking revision of history, at one verbal stroke, excised the first 30 years of Italian Communist history – when the party most assuredly believed in the Leninist one-party state, as well as the fantasy of proletarian dictatorship.

Berlinguer was also the disciple of Gramsci's successor as Italian Communist *capo*, Palmiro Togliatti, who had been a Soviet secret police commissar and architect of terror in the Spanish civil war. Indeed, he seems to have been specially prepared by Togliatti to succeed him in running the party.

The latest revelations about Berlinguer ring true. The smiling darling of the Eurointellectual set knew a lot about getting and holding power. He waited to become a Communist until the Allies arrived in Sardinia in 1943, in the aftermath of the Fascist downfall. Not for him the risks and sacrifices of the revolutionary underground. But he soon showed his sense of gratitude to the Allies by organizing bread riots in his native town.

In 1948 a great many people both in Europe and the United States feared, with considerable reason, that Italy would go the way of Czechoslovakia and become a new Soviet puppet. Whether or not the action by the Moscow dinosaurs in having a party temporarily support NATO and pluralism in the 1970s was a good one, the basic point is that the Italian Communists remained subordinate.

The Italian Communists did not become the Democratic Left until after Muscovite Communism had finally collapsed with the fall of the Berlin Wall. And the process of admitting they were consistently wrong on basic issues – including the infallibility of Stalin during the 1930s – has been slow and sporadic. The veterans of the Italian Partisan movement, for example, are squeamish about admitting their involvement in the mass murder of thousands of so-called fascists after World War II, many of whom were either innocent or innocuous. Other scholarly research and documentary releases have shown that the Italian Communists maintained their former Partisan cadres as a secret paramilitary force throughout the Cold War, fully prepared to carry out orders from Moscow to engage in renewed terror, sabotage, and civil war.

There's one more reason to dredge up the past and bring it out in the light. Many opponents of the so-called Democratic Left, including those associated with Italian conservative politician Silvio Berlusconi, say that a change in name and even an admission of past errors is not enough. The former Communists remain unchanged in their essential political habits – above all, the tendency to view their opponents as enemies, rather than as fellow participants in a consensual political process. Accompanying that is the tendency, exemplified by Berlinguer decades ago, to engage in the kind of rhetoric they think will assure them of power, while knowing in their hearts they don't mean it.

–The Wall Street Journal Europe, June 6, 2000

EPILOGUE

Confession of a Counter-Revolutionary

These concluding notes constitute reminiscence and meditation, firstly about a book. Or about books.

I love books. I read them, I collect them, I write them. Of DeQuincey it was said that having filled a flat with books, so that he could no longer move around in it, he rented another, and then another, so that at his death he was a tenant in a multiplicity of flats, all filled with books.

Something similar happened to me. My home in San Francisco became so filled with books I could not move around. I could entertain nobody; even the bed was covered with books, and I opened the doors with difficulty.

So I moved to Sarajevo, a great city for books. Sarajevo residents may grimace when they read those words...

A need for a new place to fill up with books was not the only reason I had for moving, but that, or those, are other stories... In any event, I moved to Sarajevo, bringing with me enough books that the airline forced me to repack them at the airport, on pain of a $300 charge for overweight.

Because, after all, many books cannot be had in Sarajevo. Some were burned in the recent war, by the Serbs, out of malice. Some were burned in the recent war, by the defenders of Sarajevo, because of the cold and absence of other fuel. Some were turned into paper for cigarettes, to be smoked by the defenders of Sarajevo. So I brought some books as presents for friends, who had lost them when their homes were burned, and some for my own use, knowing I could not get them otherwise.

After three months in Sarajevo, early in November 1999, I visited London. The motivation for the trip is unimportant. I stayed in Bloomsbury, in a Quaker club, with no televisions or telephones in the rooms. Plusher hotels nearby advertised antiquarian book sales, for, after all, there is no greater city for books than London. Indeed, I was happy to find my own books for sale in Charing Cross Road, some new, some used. A feeling of great validation filled me: my books are sold in London!

One night I went through one of those antiquarian book fairs and found lots of interesting books; I even bought one. No, it was not my own. The book I bought is of no importance: it was a trifle. Far more important was another book, which I did not buy.

The book I did not buy sat in the middle of a pile of travel books, which was how I found it, because I was looking for the works of Edith Durham on Albania (which I did not find.) The book I did not buy was little more than a pamphlet. But what a pamphlet! It was, in fact, a Communist pamphlet in German, promoting the new Soviet film industry, written by the great Bolshevik enlightener Anatoly Lunacharsky and published in 1929. Most of it was taken up by stills from the classics of Eisenstein and the other great Soviet cinematographers.

It was priced at £80, which I could have afforded. There was a time I would have clasped such an item to my breast, would have lovingly caressed and paged through it, staring for hours at each of the images and fantasising all I knew about Bolshevik intellectuals, about classic Soviet films, about the lost chances for the world revolution. But I did not buy that book.

I did not think how valuable that book might have been to my friends who are filmmakers and students in Sarajevo.

I did not think of the literally unbelievable crimes of the KGB outlined in *The Mitrokhin Archive* which I had bought a few hours earlier on Charing Cross Road.

I thought only, this is something I once would have treasured; but that is over for me. I no longer feel connected with it.

I did not buy that book.

*   *   *   *   *

And then it was November 30, 1999, the day the riots erupted in Seattle, a city – and a situation – I knew well, in the past. But I'm far from the street fighting, the clouds of pepper spray, the plaintive cries of golden children, and the growls of boneheaded lefties hungry for martyrdom. I walk around Bologna, the Italian town once known as "Red," as "the best managed city in Italy," where radical leftism now seems only a memory, a local item of nostalgia… About the great local administration I am unconvinced, since it seems one cannot get a taxi

179

on the street, but only by telephone order, and then one waits too long, and misses one's appointments. Imagine New York with a rule like that.

There's snow on the sidewalks but the air is delightfully clear and warm after a winter in Sarajevo. I've come to lecture on the Yugoslav war, at the Johns Hopkins overseas campus. It's my first time in Italy, after many visits to France, which seems, by comparison, an overbearing offspring of Roman culture, and Spain, the place I once loved so much, which now appears as a mere sketch of post-Roman glory. I came, I saw, I fell in love. The Alitalia stewardess was the most beautiful woman I had ever encountered, at least for a moment.

The arcaded walls of Bologna were covered with graffiti, definitely nostalgic in their import: *W* (Viva) *Ocalan, Berlinguer Pusher* (this last in English, referring to scabrous charges that the architect of "Eurocommunism" was a drug lord), *Il Communismo...* with the final words either never added or scraped off. In the Feltrinelli bookstore, a giant portrait of Lenin covered a wall. There I bought a copy of the *Communist Manifesto*, curious to reread Marx's stirring defence of global trade, while windows were broken in his memory on faraway Puget Sound. In the basement of a record store, I find a pile of plastic disks, to be played on a kind of machine that no longer exists: 400 lire each, or 20 cents, for *The Hymn of the Union of Soviet Socialist Republics*. I imagine some stubborn old factory worker playing that as he sat down to eat his pasta, glowering at his wife and children while he dreams of a great social change. But the recollection is distant, incongruous, and even a little threatening, like the footprint of a dinosaur suddenly discovered in the desert.

Two days previously, the centre-left had won the local election, but by a slimmer margin than ever before. In the previous vote, the left took Red Bologna 60-40, but now the tally is closer to 47-44. So Bologna gets pinker, and even a bit grey, politically. Local folk have had nearly enough, it seems, of the left. Yes, the ex-Communists have embraced the free market; yes, d'Alema, the former Marxist who leads the country, supported NATO on Kosovo. But, as noted elsewhere in this book, in their hearts the Italian "exes" have not changed. D'Alema caused a scandal by procuring the censorship of a cartoonist who sought to portray him frantically applying "white out" ink to a list of the Soviet spies named as active in Italy, in *The Mitrokhin Archive*. And d'Alema's use of the judiciary to hound his chief national rival, Silvio Berlusconi, with charges of corruption from many years past, leave a bad taste in everyone's mouth. Long ago service to the K.G.B. by political activists should be forgotten, it seems, but long ago payment of minor bribes by businessman, even by one's remote subordinates, cannot be forgiven.

Yet in Italy all these issues are timeless. In another bookstore, I thumbed through Caesar's *Gallic War* in a bilingual edition, reading Latin and Italian on facing pages, with the sensation that it might just have come out, the bestseller of the season, and that its author might appear in the store for a publicity event. At a newsstand a calendar featured portraits of Mussolini and fascist slogans. The tiny ultraleftist journals for sale in Feltrinelli reminded me of dead lilacs on a tomb.

I remain a Californian, wherever I may be, and so a historical chain from Mexico, from Spain, and ultimately from Italy, has meaning. I tell everyone I meet in Bologna that I come from San Francisco, named for the founder of Italian vernacular poetry, and, of course, everyone answers – as I found Italian troops in Kosovo did – that they have relatives in California, or have gone there, or cannot wait to go. Fellow diners and waiters and restaurant owners are impressed at my command of the Italian menu, little realizing that to be a San Franciscan without knowing this cooking would be like being a Londoner who could not say who William the Conqueror was or a Bostonian ignorant of St. Patrick's Day. Or a Bolognese unacquainted with Julius Caesar. The rest of the world has history; Californians have cuisine.

It is all, then, a dream for me, a surrealist dream. And the authentic end of Communism is a key element of the dream. The next morning, at the airport, I buy *Il Manifesto*, the ultraleftist daily from the '60s, and am handed its brightly hued supplement, advertising the latest cars. In Italy, some things are truly eternal.

* * * * *

But I knew that, pondering the wreckage in the streets of Seattle, American investors might fear a global revival of the extreme left. Such anxiety is, I believe, unwarranted.

First, we should be clear about the meaning of Seattle's radical remnant. Todd Gitlin, a former activist with the Students for a

Democratic Society and author of *The Sixties: Years of Hope, Days of Rage,* described it as a path-breaking alliance of environmentalists and labour, breathing new life into the historic values of socialism.

That is nonsense. The brats in Seattle revealed that the left is dead on its feet, soon to be entombed by an economy it taunts. Gitlin and other stirrers of retrograde revolution should review the same 20th century history they invoke to idealize the anarchist rebels of three generations ago. Were they to bone up on it, they would discover that the enemies of free trade and champions of protectionism were Hitler, Mussolini, and Stalin, not Emma Goldman.

And the unfortunate longshore workers of Seattle, once known for their political independence, might find out that the symbol on their placards, an octopus with a death grip on the world, is stolen from a classic source, namely the anti-Jewish iconography of the Nazis. The leftover left will grasp at any excuse to rouse the rabble and get victims marching to nowhere. As the millennium ends, the left, once eloquent, is now merely noisy.

Finally, the rioting against the global economic summit in Davos, Switzerland, at the end of January 2000, was seen by some as Round II in the international resurgence of anarchism and a further harbinger of major social unrest, provoking alarm within the global economic and political leadership. It led some politicians – notably U.S. president Bill Clinton – to emit phrases of sympathy for the rioters, whose main achievement was a violent assault on a McDonald's in the Swiss resort. More such idiocy would afflict Washington itself, during a meeting of the International Monetary Fund, and then there was London on May Day, and it seemed horribly contagious. And finally the nonsense came full circle, to Bologna where I had meditated on the nostalgia of it all, during a meeting of the Organisation for Economic Cooperation and Development, in June 2000.

For Clinton to engage in such tomfoolery should have come as no surprise. His native Arkansas has a long history of economic demagoguery by its populist politicians. Indeed, one of Clinton's predecessors, Gov. Orval Faubus, was known as an extreme socialist in the 1930s, before becoming a race-baiter in the 1950s. So urging on the mob against alleged economic tyranny by bankers and business executives came naturally to Clinton.

More serious was the panicky reaction of business leaders, haunted by the spectre of wide scale upheaval, who aver that a huge problem faces them in explaining the benefits of capitalism to the young and the angry (many of the latter being, in fact, not so young after all.)

They shouldn't bother. An examination of social history over the past two centuries offers many lessons about social radicalism, all of which suggest that the disorders at the Seattle and Davos summits, in Washington and London, discomfiting as they may be for the schedules of conference attendees, were anything but a serious threat to the modern order.

Riots and other disturbances will always break out from time to time, no matter how stable the society, because there will always be discontented, alienated people, victims of short-term economic adjustments, and aggrieved folk attempting to protect outdated economic privileges, customs and habits. In addition, there will always be political mistakes and outbursts of local temper that lead to occasional strife. But the difference between episodic social conflicts and profound, long-term radical movements is considerable. And there seems to be a kind of law of declining influence in the radical movements of the past 200 years.

The Jacobins of the French Revolution were bourgeois; they represented the triumph of the new business class over the feudal and religious structures that had ruled Europe for centuries. The socialists and anarchists that followed them, beginning in the middle third of the 19th century, based themselves on a later emerging class, the industrial workers.

The radical leftists of the 1930s also represented a newly rising class, the urban intellectuals and semi-intellectuals, who felt ill-at-ease in a capitalist society that often left them without a secure income. The protestors of the 1960s embodied the anxieties of yet another new social layer, the products of the vast expansion of college education after World War II.

But as these revolutionary movements succeeded one another they appealed to sectors of society that were further and further away from the productive core of civilization. Even the labor movement, which once inculcated radical hopes, had represented, in its time, a key element of society. But since the 1930s, radicalism has flourished in more and more marginal, less and less significant sectors of the economy. The leftist intellectuals of the 1930s were better at writing essays than at crafting economic reforms, as we see from the eventual failure of the New Deal and its parallel systems, fascism and Stalinism. The 60s rebels disrupted and degraded the universities and the broader culture but did not affect the capitalist order, except by introducing meditation rooms and cappuccino caffés onto "campuses" like that run by Microsoft. The streetfighters of Seattle, Davos, Washington, London and even Bologna are distant indeed from the reality of modern economic life; they are proud of being jobless squatters.

And as radicalism has moved away from the center of economic reality, its imagined enemy has grown more and more imaginary. The "savage" capitalism the protestors claim to aim at is a caricature out of Charles Dickens. To this day, the business class that led the French Revolution continues to bring democratic change, only rarely accompanied by conflict, to developing nations in Asia, Latin America, and Africa. For example, the democratization of the Philippines and South Korea were both impelled by the investment classes, as is the transition away from a de facto one-party state in Mexico.

The benefits of globalization are even visible in Europe. Bill Clinton, as well as the protestors to whom he panders, should ask the citizens of a southern Irish city like Limerick whether the arrival of multinational investment has been a blessing or a curse for them. Globalization has brought less, not more inequality, notwithstanding the rhetoric of economic illiterates like American union leader John J. Sweeney.

Business leaders should not get spooked over an occasional riot. They should keep a steady hand on the tiller, guiding the world to a global economy based on free trade. Either way, the business classes will continue to bring real improvement and prosperity to the peoples of the world, notwithstanding the disruptive escapades of a few ignorant radicals. The great era of social revolution ended long ago. Its decadence was manifest in the rise of Stalinism and its seduction of intellectuals. But all things have a beginning and an end, and for the left, old as well as new, there is no further horizon. The time has come to sing a new song.

–Expanded from Investors' Business Daily, December 22, 1999